Western Hemisphere Drug Policy Leadership Conference

Sponsored By:

Office of National Drug Control Policy
Executive Office of the President

International Narcotics & Law Enforcement
Department of State

Inter-American Drug Abuse Control Commission
Organization of American States

For sale by the U.S. Government Printing Office
Superintendent of Documents, Mail Stop: SSOP, Washington, DC 20402-9328
ISBN 0-16-050414-7

Table of Contents

Appendices   97

Foreword

In November 1999 an historic meeting was held in Washington to discuss drug abuse, production, and trafficking in the Americas. This first-ever *Western Hemisphere Drug Policy Leadership Conference* provided ministerial level officials an opportunity to discuss the significant counter-drug challenges that we will face in the first decade of the new millennium. It also enabled us to identify immediate measures to consolidate recent progress made in enhancing hemispheric cooperation and coordination in addressing the drug issue.

The Leadership Conference presentations were of such high quality we concluded that they should be made available broadly to government officials, academic experts and concerned members of the public. For this reason we have compiled the conference presentations into this document, which is available in both English and Spanish, both in printed form and on ONDCP's internet web site.

The Leadership Conference was held just a month after the approval of the Multilateral Evaluation Mechanism (MEM) in Montevideo in October, 1999. The establishment of the MEM signals a new stage in counter-drug cooperation within the hemisphere. Starting in calendar year 2000, every country in the Americas, under the MEM, will undergo objective evaluation by a team of multilateral technical experts. These evaluations, which are based on a series of specific performance indicators negotiated over the last 18 months, are designed to highlight the strengths and weaknesses of each nation's counter-drug efforts, with the specific goal of improving the overall effort.

Evaluation reports will be published by the Organization of American States' Inter-American Drug Abuse Control Commission (OAS/CICAD) by the end of 2000. The first year results of MEM implementation will be discussed at the Third Summit of the Americas in Quebec City, Canada in April 2001.

Because the MEM is such an important initiative, we decided to include in this report several documents on the MEM, including the complete list of performance indicators. We hope that these items, along with the substantive conference presentations that make up the bulk of the report, prove to be useful to readers. Because of the success of the first Western Hemisphere Drug Policy Leadership Conference, we expect that similar conferences will be held in the future.

Sincerely,

Barry R. McCaffrey
Director
Office of National Drug Control Policy

César Gaviria
Secretary General
Organization of American States

Conference Executive Summary

The Western Hemisphere Drug Policy Leadership Conference, organized by the Office of National Drug Control Policy (ONDCP) and the Inter-American Drug Abuse Control Commission (CICAD), was held in Washington, D.C. from November 3-5, 1999. National drug policy leaders and delegations representing 34 countries of the Americas to the Conference heard detailed presentations on a variety of drug-related topics and held comprehensive discussions on how to address new challenges in the new century. The following is a summary of the main discussion points presented:

Future Changes in Drug Use: Patterns and Trends

More widespread use of drugs throughout hemisphere—many countries now seeing significant levels of drug use for the first time.

- Globalized consumption is creating two-way trafficking – plant-based drugs going north; precursors, amphetamines, cash and designer drugs going south.

- New drug consumption patterns are emerging, including poly-drug use, in many countries.

- Increased use of drugs and alcohol among adolescent women.

- Countries reject idea of legalization, recognizing that it would considerably increase social and public health problems if drugs were socially acceptable and available freely at a low price.

Research and Science Findings: Public Health Impact of Drug Abuse and Addiction

- Addiction is a treatable brain disease, with social and behavioral aspects.

- Important to treat prisoners for drug use during imprisonment—recidivism is lower among those who receive treatment.

- Need to assist prisoners during the transition from prison back into the community.

- Treatment does not have to be voluntary to be effective—even if ordered by the addict's family or the courts, it can be beneficial.

- Research results on prevention, education and treatment should be disseminated, in appropriate languages, throughout hemisphere.

Current and Future Trends in Drug Trafficking

- Exchange of information on the importation/exportation of commercial products is essential in order to combat drug trafficking.

- Illicit drugs are now, and will continue to be, the leading source of income for organized crime groups.

- Priority must be given to the issue of money laundering—government personnel must be trained in the investigation of financial crimes and use of asset forfeiture laws.

- Need for effective coordination between the justice system and the ministries of finance, interior and other agencies working in the fight against drugs in each country.

- Importance of developing a relationship between drug investigation and control agencies and national security institutions.

- Regional intelligence training centers needed that offer courses for members of security and intelligence forces, law enforcement officials, judges, prosecutors, etc.

- INTERPOL support and financing for the establishment of regional centers is fundamental for an efficient intelligence system to combat drug trafficking.

Law Enforcement Strategies for the Future

- Every nation needs set of laws which provides ability, under rule of law, to conduct investigations of drug trafficking, money laundering, and corruption.

- Globalization of drug trade requires cooperation—need for interdependence, increased collaboration, more rapid exchange of information and intelligence,

- Creation of regional databases and greater use of technology.

- Evaluating what new technical capabilities are required by governments (CICAD might play a role in evaluating what is needed).

Social and Economic Costs of Drugs

- Measuring the cost of drugs and their social, economic and political impact is important to design an effective anti-drug strategy.

- Knowing these drug cost implications is essential for government decision-making and allocation of resources as well as to raise social awareness.

- Trial guidelines for evaluating costs have been established (in Canada) and are being tested and adapted to different situations.

- Cross-disciplinary research (for example among economists, policy-advisors, researchers) must be increased.

Future Challenges to Drug Control Policy

- Today's traffickers are savvy marketers and business experts—they are diversifying product line, exploiting new markets, introducing synthetic drugs and involving themselves in a broader array of criminal activities.

- Need to reward and protect individuals who reveal corruption and to conduct public audits on expenditure of drug-related government funds.

- Must make sure justice system as whole works—cannot just arrest people—must have strong prosecutors and judges as well as effective prison system.

- Nations should work together, creating national & international systems, & inter-agency coordination.

- Priority should be set in safeguarding the individual from dangers posed by drugs.

- A positive policy on drugs must be developed, informing people of the dangers of drugs, and in so doing earn the support of the community.

- Achieving hemispheric cooperation is fundamental in areas such as technology, information, science, health, education, legislative and judicial cooperation.

The Multilateral Evaluation Mechanism

- MEM is historic achievement—no large group of nations has ever attempted such a multifaceted mutual evaluation system.

- CICAD and participating nations will learn a lot in first year, 2000. We must apply lessons for 2001 MEM process.

- Year 2000 results will be reported to Heads of Government in Quebec City at the 3rd Summit of the Americas.

- MEM should help focus National Governments—many nations need to develop technical capacity to measure consumption, to provide quality treatment, to control drug and chemical trafficking and address money laundering.

- Policy makers in each country can only make informed decision with good data—MEM will help to provide that data.

Agreements

The following agreements were reached during the Conference:

- Alternative measures for minor drug offenses should be discussed at the next CICAD meeting.

- The next Western Hemisphere Drug Policy Leadership Conference will be incorporated into a future CICAD meeting.

Presentations

Western Hemisphere Drug Policy Leadership Conference

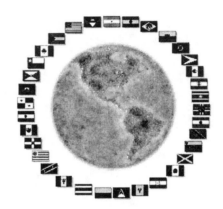

Washington, D.C.

November 3-5, 1999

I: Introductory Remarks

Thomas Pickering, Under Secretary of State for Political Affairs, United States

Biography

On May 27, 1997, Thomas R. Pickering was sworn in as Under Secretary of State for Political Affairs. He holds the personal rank of Career Ambassador, the highest in the United States Foreign Service. He previously served as Ambassador to the Russian Federation from May 1993 until November 1996. He also served as Ambassador to India from 1992-1993, Permanent Representative to the United Nations from 1989-1992, Ambassador to Israel from 1985-1988, Ambassador to El Salvador from 1983-1985, and Ambassador to Nigeria from 1981-1983. He was Assistant Secretary for Oceans and International Environmental and Scientific Affairs from 1978 to 1981. From 1974 until 1978, Ambassador Pickering was the United States Ambassador to the Hashemite Kingdom of Jordan. Thomas Pickering was born on November 5, 1931, in Orange, New Jersey. He received a Bachelor's Degree in 1953 from Bowdoin College in Brunswick, Maine, cum laude, with high honors in history. In 1954, he attended the Fletcher School of Law and Diplomacy at Tufts University and received a Master's Degree. He was awarded a Fulbright Scholarship to the University of Melbourne and received a second Master's Degree in 1956. From 1956 to 1959, he was on active duty in the United States Navy and later served in the Naval Reserve to the grade of Lieutenant Commander.

Western Hemisphere Cooperation in Fighting the Scourge of Narcotics

Remarks by Under Secretary Pickering
Western Hemisphere Drug Leadership Conference
November 3, 1999 - New Heights Restaurant

Director McCaffrey, Mr. Beall, thank you for inviting me to this evening's dinner and for the opportunity to comment on the important work we are doing together to reduce and ultimately to eliminate the narcotics problem.

On the eve of a new millennium, with all the promise and excitement that inspires, this is a very fitting time to bring together senior counternarcotics officials in the Western Hemisphere. Your leadership is essential as we confront the gravest of threats to our citizens, our societies and the security of our nations in the 21st Century.

The narcotics control spotlight has shone particularly brightly on the Western Hemisphere in recent years because this hemisphere has acknowledged what is truly at stake from the drug threat and has responded with an increasingly cooperative broad-based approach that is working. That is what I would like to focus my comments on this evening—without losing sight of the significant challenges that still lie ahead.

To have an effective anti-drug effort, we need a balanced approach with shared responsibilities. The nations of this hemisphere have responded collectively to this challenge with the unprecedented creation of the Multilateral Evaluation Mechanism (MEM) endorsed last month in Montevideo.

The MEM is a remarkable accomplishment of which we should all be proud. It is the most concrete manifestation yet of our willingness to address the drug problem through multilateral cooperation. Narcotics trafficking is simply too large, too complex, and too fluid a problem to be tackled by any one country or small group of countries. Moreover, the damage drug abuse and trafficking does to any one of us in the region eventually hurts us all. The United States welcomes the opportunity to be among the first countries to have its strategy reviewed by this process. We think we will have a great deal to learn and to share through this assessment.

The MEM negotiations were so successful because, among, other reasons, we as a region had narcotics control momentum on our side. Our negotiations occurred against the backdrop of encouraging trends that helped create a positive, can-do atmosphere. From controlling illicit drug crop cultivation to reducing illicit drug use, this hemisphere has made gains that were unimaginable a few years ago.

Illicit coca cultivation in 1998 was at the lowest levels since the region began making scientifically-based estimates over a dozen years ago. Where we have been able to put all the elements in place for a comprehensive crop control strategy—including developing long-term plans, securing funding for alternative development, and instituting enforcement programs—cultivation of illegal crops has plummeted and alternative legitimate crops increased.

We face new challenges as traffickers adapt to our successes, but with continued regional solidarity we will ultimately triumph.

The tide is also shifting against the region's most feared drug syndicates. In their attacks on judicial and legislative bodies, assaults on the media, penetration of banking and other financial institutions, these organizations began to symbolize more than just drug-running criminals. They represented an attack on democracy, human rights, and the rule of law that none of us were willing to tolerate any longer.

We have responded with a sustained effort that is paying dividends. Thanks to elaborate regional efforts to pool information on these organizations and to coordinate operations against them, authorities have dismantled the most notorious groups, including—and this is especially important—much of their region-wide support apparatus. With each success, the trafficking organizations grow weaker, the authorities stronger, and the narcotics control field more level.

None of these positive steps would mean much, however, if drug abuse continued to soar. Demand reduction, I believe, is the ultimate objective of all our counternarcotics strategies; in the end, this is how we measure the success of any of our programs.

The United States, as one of the world's largest and most lucrative illicit drug markets, has taken the requirement to reduce its levels of illegal drug consumption seriously. General McCaffrey will tell you that this is the top priority of our national drug control strategy. A snapshot at any point in time will show that the United States has a serious drug abuse problem. Two snapshots however, will show that we are making important progress. Most significantly, we have cut cocaine use from 5.7 million users in 1985 to 1.5 million users currently—a 70 percent reduction.

These achievements, however, come at a time when cocaine use elsewhere in the world, including Latin America, is rising. We must take advantage of opportunities to work outside the confines of government institutions and connect with families, the media, public interest groups, and other nongovernmental organizations that can help deliver drug prevention and rehabilitation programs to those who are most at risk and victimized by drug abuse.

None of these observations should make us complacent. Indeed, trafficking patterns are already shifting in ways that warrant our strong, coordinated response.

One of the most pressing situations is the rapid expansion of coca cultivation in the guerrilla-dominated areas of Colombia. Under guerrilla protection, coca cultivation has more than doubled in the past four years, giving Colombia the world's largest crop. The growth has nearly offset unprecedented reductions in coca cultivation elsewhere in Colombia and the rest of the region.

Few countries have faced the type of narcotics and insurgent challenge that Colombia now encounters. The insurgents probably earn at least $30-$40 million a year from the drug trade, money they plow back into weapons, recruitment, and expanded operations. No one however, is more aware of the stakes than Colombia itself, and it is responding with a comprehensive strategy and operational plan to break the narcotics-guerrilla nexus, produce peace with the insurgents, advance economic and judicial reforms, and achieve a complete, permanent, elimination of coca cultivation.

We are working to find the resources to make Colombia's strategy work. But this must be a regional effort to be truly effective. We must all work to ensure Colombia's success and to prevent traffickers from simply displacing cultivation one area to another.

The fragmentation of trafficking patterns throughout the region in reaction to the break-up of the major syndicates is another area of concern. For a time, Mexican-based organizations were best poised to connect producers and markets. Indeed, the largest cocaine flows in the world are now probably traveling from South America, through Mexico, and into the United States. The United States and Mexico are working to address this threat through a series of high-level contact groups, but more than our interests are at stake.

We can also expect other traffickers in the hemisphere to try to capitalize on opportunities occasioned by the realignment of trafficking organizations. This could result in processing operations proliferating across the hemisphere followed by the emergence of relatively small, but nonetheless internationally-connected organizations associated with these processing operations.

The result could be a surge in cocaine availability and certainly a dispersion of routes and methods as drugs begin flowing from so many sources. This is not a prediction, but a warning about one scenario that could happen if we do not sustain and broaden our effort. It underscores that there is much we still have to achieve collectively.

We also need to bring other alternative development donors to the table. Just last week, General McCaffrey was delivering this message to the Europeans, who can clearly do more in this regard.

And all of us must continue to strengthen across-the-board our domestic narcotics control institutions from those that focus on demand reduction and seek to inoculate the most at risk-populations by providing information, prevention and rehabilitation programs, and positive alternatives to the drug culture, to the judicial institutions that must disarm traffickers of their most potent weapon—corruption—and assemble the means by which the police and courts can work in tandem to effectively attack the full range of narcotics-related crimes.

This is a week for moving forward, for building on success, and for, thinking creatively about how to adapt lessons learned and to apply new approaches to the most intractable narcotics control challenges.

By striving for excellence in our own anti-drug efforts, each of us is contributing to a genuine alliance that will be far greater than the sum of its individual parts. This is a true partnership and reflects an unprecedented level of mutual trust and confidence in the future. It will serve as a model for other regions and for the global community. Only as true partners working together on all fronts can we hope to meet and effectively beat back the daunting global drug challenge.

I feel privileged to be working with and within the august group that I see assembled here tonight and am greatly heartened by this success. To that end and effort, I pledge full USG support and participation. Again, thank you for inviting me to join you tonight and thank you for the efforts each of you is making to eliminate this scourge.

You here tonight hold the future in your hands. Your skill, dedication, vision, and courage will not only make our children safer, they will also safeguard our democracies and economies. Thank you very much for your work and sacrifice.

II: Director's Opening Remarks

Barry R. McCaffrey, Director, Office of National Drug Control Policy, United States

Biography

Barry McCaffrey was confirmed by unanimous vote of the U.S. Senate as the Director of the White House Office of National Drug Control Policy (ONDCP) on 29 February 1996. He serves as a member of the President's Cabinet, the President's Drug Policy Council, and the National Security Council for drug-related issues. Barry McCaffrey graduated from Phillips Academy in Andover, Massachusetts and the U.S. Military Academy. He holds a Master of Arts degree in civil government from American University and taught American government, national security studies, and comparative politics at West Point. He attended Harvard University's National Security Program. He is a member of the Council on Foreign Relations and an associate member of the Inter-American Dialogue.

Among the honors he has received are: the Department of State's Superior Honor Award for the Strategic Arms Limitation Talks; the Norman E. Zinberg Award of the Harvard Medical School; the Founders Award of the American Academy of Addiction Psychiatry; the NAACP Roy Wilkins Renown Service Award; the National Drug Prevention League National Leadership Award; and decorations from France, Brazil, Argentina, Colombia, Peru, and Venezuela.

Prior to confirmation as ONDCP Director, he was the Commander-in-Chief of the U.S. Armed Forces Southern Command coordinating national security operations in Latin America. During his career, he served overseas for thirteen years, which included four combat tours: Dominican Republic, Vietnam (twice), and Iraq. At retirement from active duty, he was the most highly decorated and youngest four star general in the U.S. Army. He twice received the Distinguished Service Cross, the nation's second highest medal for valor. He also was awarded three Purple Heart medals for wounds sustained in combat. During Operation Desert Storm, he commanded the 24th Infantry Division and led the 370-kilometer "left hook" attack into the Euphrates River Valley. General McCaffrey served as the JCS assistant to General Colin Powell and supported the Chairman as the staff advisor to the Secretary of State and the U.S. Ambassador to the United Nations.

DIRECTOR'S OPENING REMARKS AT THE
DRUG POLICY LEADERSHIP CONFERENCE
NOVEMBER 4, 1999

Let me take this opportunity to welcome to the Western Hemisphere Drug Policy Leadership Conference the Heads of Delegations from throughout the Americas. We are pleased that you and your delegations could travel to Washington for what we expect will be an historic meeting. We owe thanks to David Beall, Executive Secretary CICAD for his tremendous leadership, not only in support of this conference, but also throughout the year. CICAD has grown to be one of the most important and effective international organizations in the world.

It is my pleasure to welcome Rand Beers, Assistant Secretary of State for International Narcotic and Law Enforcement Affairs, head of the U.S. Delegation to this conference. He is joined by representatives of the: Department of Justice, Drug Enforcement Administration, Federal Bureau of Investigations, Department of the Treasury, Customs Service, Financial Crimes Enforcement Network, National Security Council, National Institute of Drug Abuse and the Departments of Education and Transportation.

The hemisphere has truly made historic progress in its combined efforts against drugs. The senior drug policy officials here today, representing their governments, have laid the groundwork for a Hemispheric Alliance Against Drugs through 5 years of hard work. This Alliance, was built through a series of important events and agreements, including:

- ◆ Narcotics Action Plan at Summit of the Americas in Miami, Florida—1994.
- ◆ Summit of the Americas Ministerial Conference on Money Laundering in Buenos Aires, Argentina—1995.
- ◆ OAS Hemispheric Anti-Drug Strategy in Montevideo, Uruguay—1996.
- ◆ OAS/CICAD 40 Action Items for Implementation of Hemispheric Strategy—1997.
- ◆ Second Summit of the Americas in Santiago, Chile—1998.

The Santiago Summit of the Americas in April 1998 was a key turning point. At the Summit, 34 Presidents made illegal drugs a top issue for the hemisphere. Our Presidents tasked CICAD to create the Multilateral Evaluation Mechanism (MEM). Over the past 18 months OAS/CICAD negotiated the MEM, under leadership of Canada (Jean Fournier) and Chile (Pablo Lagos). The MEM was signed in Montevideo, Uruguay on October 5, 1999. The MEM will use technical experts from each of the 34 countries to evaluate counterdrug performance of every nation in the hemisphere, *including the United States.*

A true Hemispheric Alliance Against Drugs has been forged. We have put behind us years of finger pointing and playing the blame game. Every nation in the hemisphere has a drug consumption and drug trafficking problem and is committed to doing something about it. Every nation has national drug coordinating body (like ONDCP) which seeks effective, workable solutions. We all understand that there is no choice but to work together against powerful drug trafficking organization which do not respect national borders.

Our intent is that this week's Western Hemisphere Drug Policy Leadership Conference will address the new counter-drug environment already emerging. Increased drug consumption in now a challenge for the entire hemisphere, with consumption growing sharply in many areas of South America. Major cities, such as Caracas, Rio, Buenos Aires, and Lima are facing drug-related problems we have long seen in Miami, New York, Los Angeles and other U.S. cities. The United States, although still a major consumer of illicit drugs, has seen cocaine consumption fall 70% over 15 years. However, we are witnessing growing use of synthetic drugs, including highly addictive methamphetamine. In Europe both the price of cocaine and its consumption rates are increasing. These new trends have led drug traffickers to develop new routes and techniques to move drugs, chemicals, and money around the globe.

These new challenges need to be addressed through cooperative efforts. We have made a good start with the development of the MEM, but we have our work cut out for us. Traffickers have tremendous resources at their disposal. However, governments also have tools and techniques that, properly applied, can make a difference.

Recent scientific advances have the potential to help all of us address our drug problems more effectively. Technology will also assist government authorities in detecting drug trafficking over land, sea and air. New capabilities are coming on line over the next two years, including the Relocatable Over-The-Horizon Radar (ROTHR) in Puerto Rico and the Amazon Surveillance System (SIVAM) in Brazil. Through Forward Operating Location (FOLs) the U.S. will continue to provide support to interdiction efforts in the Andean region as well as the transit zone.

Dynamic advances in the science of addiction are already assisting us in developing more effective tools for treatment and prevention. Dr. Alan Leshner, Director of the National Institute of Drug Abuse, will demonstrate through advanced scanning technologies how drug consumption changes the brain and how we are learning to reverse these changes.

This Drug Policy Leadership Conference will enable us to explore all of these changing trends and to learn from each nation's experiences. The participation of all the delegations is the key to success of the conference. We have asked presenters to kick off the conversation, but we are looking to the delegations to contribute their views and perspectives. The work we are doing, both here today and within each of our countries, is challenging, but we have already made tremendous progress. By continuing to work closely together, as one hemisphere united against drugs, we will make a difference. Thank you very much.

III: Future Changes in Drug Use: Patterns and Trends

Augusto Perez Gomez, Director, President's Program to Confront Drug Consumption, Colombia

Biography

As of October 1998, Augusto Perez Gomez has served as Director of the Presidential Program 'RUMBOS' to address drug consumption in Colombia. He was born in Bogotá, Colombia on May 25, 1947. Perez has previously served as a Psychologist of the National University of Colombia and as an Expert in Group Dynamics for the University of Puerto Rico. Perez earned a Masters and Ph.D. in Psychology at the Lovaina Belgian University and the 'Chargé d'Enseignement' Faculté Libres des Lettres et Sciences Humaines, Lille, Francia (1974). He served as a Visiting Professor School of Medicine at Chelsea and Westminster, London University (1994) and as a Full Professor, University of the Andes, Bogotá. Perez is the author of seven books and 114 articles in English, Spanish and French. He won the National Clinical Psychology Award in 1987 and the National Clinical Psychology Award in 1992.

CHALLENGES 2000-2010

PROGRAM OFFICE OF THE PRESIDENT OF THE REPUBLIC OF COLOMBIA

This presentation will focus exclusively on drug use for two reasons. Firstly, drug use is almost always the "Cinderella" of the drug issue. Secondly, since the President of the Republic of Colombia decided just over one month ago to separate supply- and demand-related functions, it would be unwise for me to give a presentation about a topic on which I am not an expert.

Changes in patterns

♦ Increased use and drop in the price of heroine.
♦ Overall increase in use among adolescent women.
♦ Lower starting age.
♦ Increased use of benzodiazepines.
♦ 'Banalization' of marijuana use.
♦ Overall increase in alcohol use.

Let's look at some of the changes in drug use patterns that we are likely to see in the coming years in Latin America:

♦ Increased use and drop in the price of heroin: this trend already exists, and heroin continues to become more widely available.

♦ Overall increase in use among adolescent women, who for a variety of reasons have joined the race in areas both good and bad.

♦ Lower starting age, a trend which has been observed for several years.

♦ Increased use of benzodiazepines: this is one of the most recent and problematic trends, since it requires medical care that is often not available.

♦ 'Banalization' of marijuana use: there is a clear trend towards an increase in marijuana use and social acceptance of the drug, ignoring or disregarding the increasingly clear findings on the negative effects of marijuana use.

♦ Overall increase in alcohol use: although commonplace in Latin America, use in women has risen markedly, particularly among women between ages 14 and 22.

♦ Drop in the use of coca paste (basuco): There is already a downward trend in upper-middle-class youth and students in general. However, I think that this good news has less to do with the effectiveness of our prevention systems, than with the devastating effects of coca paste use.

♦ Risk of increased use of synthetic substances: these substances are readily available, even though people often do not know what they are.

♦ Risk of increased use of depressants: same as above.

♦ Rise in problems related to intravenous substances, particularly HIV: we run the risk of repeating the history of cocaine, with the added difficulty that we do not know how to manage this type of problem, either technically or in terms of available infrastructure and resources.

Issues for Further Discussion:

♦ Less emphasis on the image of drug users as "irresponsible sick people".
♦ Increase in some measures that are part of the 'damage prevention' policy.
♦ Clarification of the conditions under which users must be accused of offenses.

These three points involve changes to the theoretical conception and therapeutic approach that will hopefully be the subject of in-depth discussion. For many years we have held mere possibilities as indisputable truths; and we have lived in awe of the idea of 'damage reduction', as if it only meant handing out syringes without rhyme or reason, when in reality this broad concept covers areas ranging from pursuit of total abstinence to establishing protections to prevent inveterate users from dying from diseases such as the different forms of hepatitis, AIDS, or other infections.

♦ Opening the debate on legalization on a more solid foundation than the economic scope of drug trafficking.
♦ Correcting errors in current laws.
♦ Regulating the operation of treatment centers.

Proponents of legalization, in most cases, have an extremely simplistic view of the drug problem. I think that we are ready to engage in in-depth discussions, allowing us to adopt joint positions and promote policies aimed not so much at suppressing and punishing users as at requiring them to assume responsibility for their behavior and its consequences. Most of the laws in the Hemisphere on this topic are contradictory; they are based on proposals made without consulting experts on the issue and disseminate definitions dropped over two decades ago.

Regulating treatment centers is of the highest priority, not only because of the damage that can be caused in many of them to persons and families that already have enough problems, but also because the proliferation of such centers is probably due to economic rather than humanitarian interests or to therapists fulfilling their personal ambitions in a role for which they are completely unprepared. For example, in many countries in the Hemisphere, it is believed that being a former drug addict is sufficient experience to become a therapist. That is like suggesting that one only has to have undergone surgery for a severe physical problem to qualify as a surgeon.

♦ Decision to support projects aimed at determining the socioeconomic costs of psychoactive substance use.
♦ International measures for the exchange of information, technology, mutual support, and joint projects.

In these two points, international cooperation is key. Through cooperation, not only can technical and methodological difficulties be resolved; it will also be easier to get policy makers to agree, since they will be accessing the same kind of relevant information.

♦ All the countries in the Hemisphere adopt similar measures to be able to evaluate intervention strategies. A decision is taken on the 'basic minimum' that must be observed in all countries in the Hemisphere in prevention, treatment, and reintegration into society.

I think that we have already started down this path while respecting our differences and individual identities. By identifying collective evaluation mechanisms and indicating basic minimum requirements we will be contributing the first building blocks for an authentic hemispheric demand prevention policy, which seems desirable given acceptance of the guidelines adopted by the United Nations.

Challenges
- Stop the rise in heroin use.
- Identify collective research strategies to make findings comparable.
- Raise the starting age.
- Involve the population in taking preventive measures.

It is easier to list the challenges than to say how we are going to achieve them; in these slides you can see that we have alternating difficult and less difficult challenges: for one and three we only have vague ideas, for now; but for two and four I am certain that sufficient progress has been made, although they still require further precision and agreements.

- Call on adolescents to change their view of psychoactive substance use.
- Develop new research strategies.
- Develop new prevention programs adapted to Latin America.

Adolescent women must receive our full attention. Not only do they exhibit one of the most troubling trends with regard to our future development; they can also play an extraordinarily positive role controlling their male friends. However, these women do not do so, because today we talk about total 'equality' even in misguided criteria and dubious conduct, as if there were some advantage to behaving foolishly.

In research, the time has come for innovation and creativity, instead of imitation at any cost. Science is not rigid or restricted to just a few possibilities: we are the ones who prefer to stick to what we already know, instead of taking risks to open up new horizons. Later I will give a concrete example of what we are doing in Colombia to resolve the problem of household studies on use.

Finally, after over 20 years of work in this field, I am firmly convinced that prevention requires respect for basic cultural conditions. Thus we know (we are not guessing, this has been tested) that in many or all countries in Latin America, young people reject rigid "manual-in-hand" prevention models that are not interactive. Consequently, those models do not work.

Strategies should be geared towards:
- Increasing participation of common citizens.
- Strengthening community values.
- Empowering the population.
- Developing new research strategies that are simple and effective.

I do not think there are any great discrepancies with regard to what I have said here. Much more should probably be added; however it boils down to this: it does not matter how many thousand experts work on prevention, or how wise they are. As long as parents, teachers, and common people do not tackle the issue personally as a priority, we will never be able to solve this problem.

III: Future Changes in Drug Use: Patterns and Trends

Jorge Bolivar Diaz C. M.D, M.P.H., Assistant Executive Secretary, SECCATID, Guatemala

Biography

Dr. Jorge Bolivar Diaz is the Executive Undersecretary, Executive Secretariat, Commission Against Drug Addiction and Illicit Drug Trafficking (SECCATID), which falls under the Vice-presidency of the Republic of Guatemala. He earned an M.D. from the University of San Carlos of Guatemala. Diaz has received a Fulbright Fellowship in Substance Abuse Institute of International Education, Johns Hopkins University, Baltimore Maryland, USA. He has also earned a Masters in Public Health from Johns Hopkins University in Baltimore, Maryland, USA.

FUTURE CHALLENGES
CHANGES IN PATTERNS OF DRUG USE AND ASSOCIATED BEHAVIORS

JORGE BOLÍVAR DÍAZ C. M.D, M.P.H. - ASSISTANT EXECUTIVE SECRETARY
SECCATID - GUATEMALA

SUMMARY OF RECENT THREATS

- Increase in drug production, trafficking and consumption.

- Recent increases in tranquilizer, amphetamine and designer drug consumption.

- Trafficking in chemical precursors not yet well controlled.

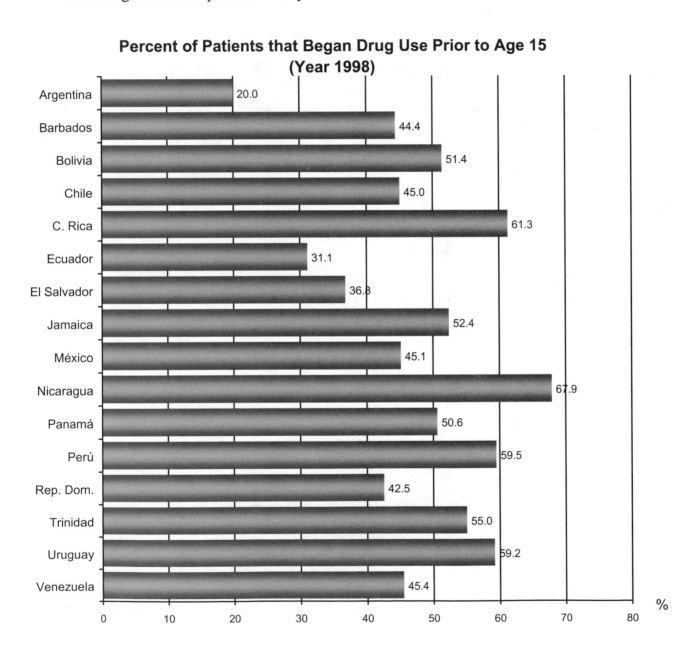

Percent of Patients that Began Drug Use Prior to Age 15 (Year 1998)

Country	%
Argentina	20.0
Barbados	44.4
Bolivia	51.4
Chile	45.0
C. Rica	61.3
Ecuador	31.1
El Salvador	36.8
Jamaica	52.4
México	45.1
Nicaragua	67.9
Panamá	50.6
Perú	59.5
Rep. Dom.	42.5
Trinidad	55.0
Uruguay	59.2
Venezuela	45.4

ACHIEVEMENTS

- National, regional and hemispheric diagnosis of the drug problem, in different areas.
- Different levels of development of national plans, incorporating community participation.
- Trained, skilled personnel in almost every country.
- Establishment of bi-national, regional, hemispheric and global agreements.
- Establishment of expert groups in the hemisphere to address the problem and identifying solutions.
- Increased support from the international community.
- Adoption of the MEM.
- Increased success in supply control.

"but the problem persists and increases ....."

WHY THE PROBLEM PERSISTS

- Epidemiological research is not adequately used, there are changes in trends and appearance of new drugs.
- Lack of studies on the personal and social impact of the drug problem.
- Low motivation or skill level of people in key leadership positions.
- Lack of political support in some regions or countries.
- Other priorities (health, education, infrastructure).
- Lack of awareness of the problem on social and political levels.
- Institutional rivalry, including governmental, non-governmental, international organizations producing such outcomes as:
    - Dispersion of resources
    - Duplication of efforts
    - Low credibility among the population
    - Collaboration and cooperation are rare
- Lack of evaluation systems of prevention and other interventions.
- Sovereignty and border problems.

CHALLENGES

- Reinforce epidemiological research in all areas with improved research instruments.
- Define skill level required for demand reduction professionals.
- Provide ongoing training.
- Define basic criteria for demand reduction efforts at the national, regional and hemispheric levels
- Disseminate research findings to key policy makers at the political and executive level
- Integrate demand reduction programs with others including health, education, infrastructure, etc.
- Integrate all organizations in common plan to achieve.
- Optimization of resources.
- One unified message.
- Cooperative and collaborative mechanisms.
- Continue with the establishment of multinational agreements in cooperation and collaboration on the drug issue.
- The Central American experience (CCP).
- Narco-activity.

For the year 2003
A common objective: "to significantly decrease all forms of drug abuse in the hemisphere"

THE GREAT CHALLENGE IS
CORDINATION

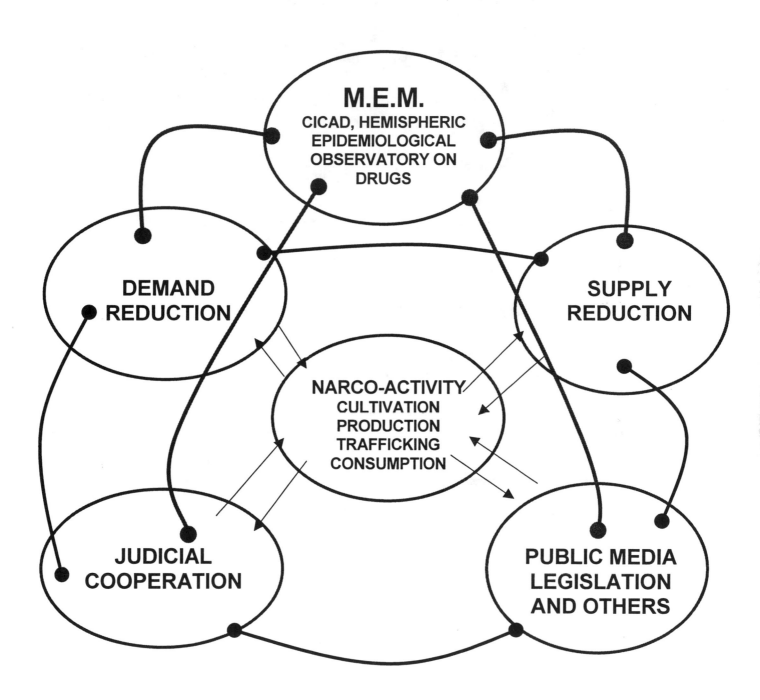

CULTIVOS DE HOJA DE COCA (OEA/CICAD/CICDAT/98)

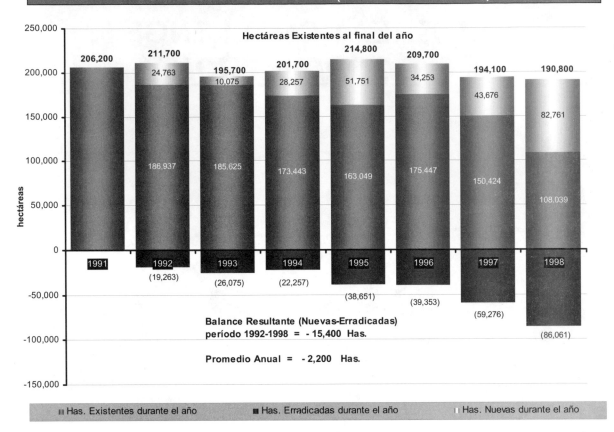

Hectáreas Existentes al final del año

Balance Resultante (Nuevas-Erradicadas)
período 1992-1998 = - 15,400 Has.

Promedio Anual = - 2,200 Has.

Has. Existentes durante el año · Has. Erradicadas durante el año · Has. Nuevas durante el año

DECOMISOS DE COCAINA (OEA/CICAD/CICDAT/98)

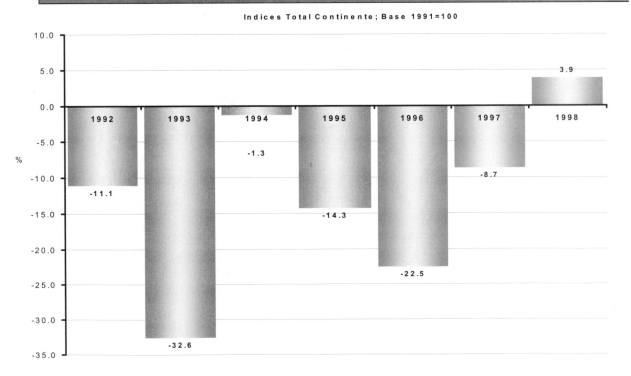

Indices Total Continente; Base 1991=100

DECOMISO DE COCAINA POR REGION (OEA/CICAD/CICDAT/98)

1994

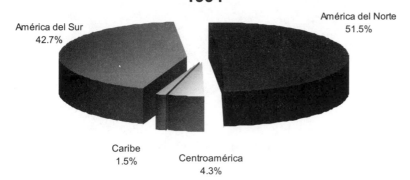

América del Sur
42.7%

América del Norte
51.5%

Caribe
1.5%

Centroamérica
4.3%

1998

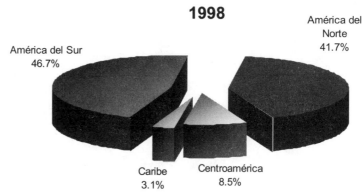

América del Sur
46.7%

América del
Norte
41.7%

Caribe
3.1%

Centroamérica
8.5%

IV: Research and Science: Public Health Impact of Drug Abuse and Addiction

Alan Leshner, Director, National Institute on Drug Abuse (NIDA), United States

Biography

Dr. Alan Leshner was appointed Director of the National Institute on Drug Abuse (NIDA) in February 1994. One of the scientific institutes of the U.S. National Institutes of Health, NIDA supports over 85% of the world's research on the health aspects of drug abuse and addiction. Prior to coming to NIDA, Dr. Leshner had been the Deputy Director and Acting Director of the National Institute of Mental Health (NIMH). He went to NIMH from the National Science Foundation (NSF), where he held a variety of senior positions focussing on basic research in the biological, behavioral and social sciences and on science education. Dr. Leshner went to NSF after 10 years at Bucknell University. Dr. Leshner has been elected a fellow of many professional societies and has received numerous awards from both professional and lay groups for his national leadership in science, mental illness and mental health, and substance abuse and addiction. In 1996, President Clinton conferred the Presidential Distinguished Executive Rank Award on Dr. Leshner, the highest award in Federal Service.

Drug Abuse and Addiction

⇒ Drug abuse and addiction are among the most complex phenomena we have ever encountered

⇒ Drug abuse and addiction are both social and public health issues

⇒ Science provides tools to manage this problem

⇒ Advances in science have revolutionized our fundamental views of drug abuse and addiction

Drug abuse is a preventable behavior.
Drug addiction is a treatable disease.

- Partnership for a Drug Free America

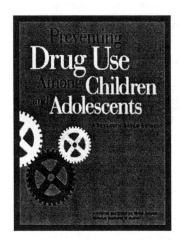

⇒ Science has taught us some of the fundamental principles that are important for drug abuse prevention

⇒ We've identified some of the fundamental principles that are important for drug abuse treatment

⇒ Why do people take drugs in the first place?

Drug Abuse Risk Factors

Community

Peer cluster

Family

Individual

Drug abuse

Drug/alcohol related traffic accidents

Delinquency

Community

Peer cluster

Family

Individual

Sexually Transmitted Diseases (including HIV/AIDS)

Academic failure and dropping out of school

Suicidal behavior

Juvenile depression

Unwanted pregnancies

Running away from home

IT'S NOT JUST ABOUT RISK

People take drugs to:

1. Feel good (sensation seeking)

2. Feel better (self-medicating)

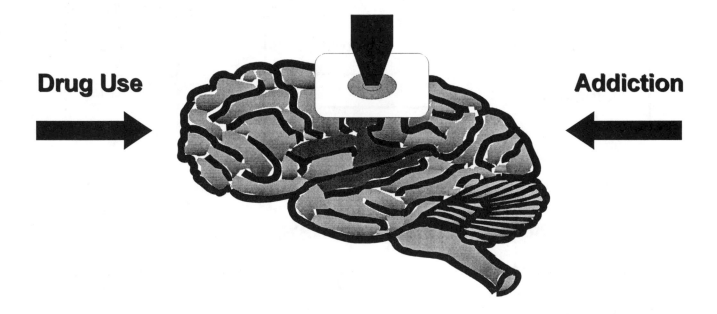

Drug Use →   ← **Addiction**

⇒ A major reason people take a drug is they like what it does to their <u>brains</u>

⇒ Prolonged drug use changes the brain in fundamental and long-lasting ways

⇒ Addiction is, fundamentally, a brain disease

Addiction is not just a brain disease

Addiction is a brain disease with imbedded behavioral and social context aspects

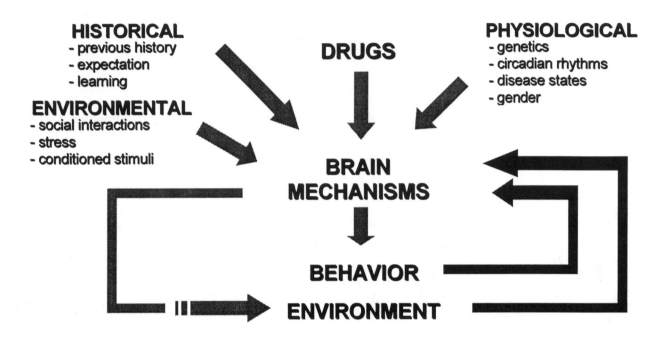

HISTORICAL
- previous history
- expectation
- learning

ENVIRONMENTAL
- social interactions
- stress
- conditioned stimuli

DRUGS

PHYSIOLOGICAL
- genetics
- circadian rhythms
- disease states
- gender

BRAIN MECHANISMS

BEHAVIOR

ENVIRONMENT

What are the implications of this concept?

⇒ We must face the fact that we are dealing with people whose brains have been changed by drugs

⇒ A major task for drug treatment is *changing brains back*!

⇒ Addiction is a biobehavioral disorder

⇒ The most effective treatment strategies will attend to <u>all</u> aspects of addiction:

    ♦ Biology

    ♦ Behavior

    ♦ Social context

It's foolish not to treat addicts while they are in prison!

This is all great! ..... BUT

⇒ There is a unique <u>Disconnect</u> between the scientific facts and the public's perception about drug abuse and addiction

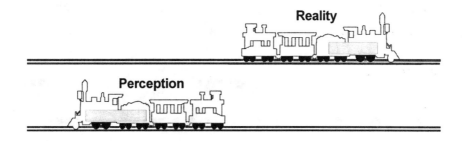

⇒ If we are going to make any real progress, we need to overcome the "Great Disconnect"

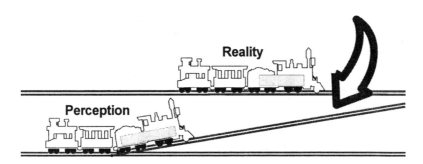

⇒ We now have the science base---Science <u>can</u> replace ideology as the foundation for drug abuse and addiction prevention, treatment, and policy strategies

INTERNATIONAL PARTNERSHIPS PLAY A KEY ROLE IN ACHIEVING OUR GOALS

INVEST Program Components:

⇒ **Post-Doctoral Research Fellowship**

⇒ **Technical Consultation**

⇒ **International Research Collaboration**

⇒ **Scientific Exchange**

⇒ **Information Dissemination**

NIDA INFORMATION DISSEMINATION

NIDA Web Page

WWW.NIDA.NIH.GOV
WWW.DRUGABUSE.GOV

National Clearinghouse for Alcohol and Drug Information (NCADI)

1-800-729-6686
in MD and DC area: 301-468-2600

NIDA Infofax
(English and Spanish)
1-888-NIH-NIDA
1-888-TTY-NIDA

V: Anti-Drug Media Campaigns

Shona Seifert, Senior Partner, Ogilvy & Mather, United States

Biography

Shona has worked for Ogilvy & Mather for 16 years. At Ogilvy's London office she was responsible for strategic development and integrated communications programs for the World Wildlife Fund. Shona also developed and managed advertising and stakeholder communications for Shell UK Oil. For 6 years Shona was the Client Service Director at Ogilvy & Mather Singapore, serving clients across Asia-Pacific. She developed an entry strategy for Kimberly-Clark's infant care business in China, ran "Emerging Market" seminars for multinational companies entering India and assisted Singapore volunteer organizations in developing education programs for orphan children in Myanmar and Vietnam. Shona also worked with Nestlé to help educate Chinese parents on the nutritional benefits of milk. Since relocating to Ogilvy & Mather in New York in 1992, Shona has guided Ogilvy agencies in South Africa and the Philippines in developing grass roots programs for teenage girls in rural areas, consulted with National Heart, Lung and Blood Institute (NHLBI) on their recent branding initiative. Shona led the Ogilvy team's response to ONDCP's Request for Proposal for the National Youth Anti-Drug Media Campaign advertising contract and is Project Director for the campaign.

The National Youth Anti-Drug Media Campaign
Presentation to:
Western Hemisphere Drug Policy Leadership Conference, Washington, DC- November 4 1999

"Alianza. La Anti Droga"

Agenda

1. Our approach to campaign design.
2. What makes this campaign unique?
3. What messages are likely to work best?
4. Who do we partner with to be successful?
5. How do we measure and sustain success?

Campaign Design

- We all face similar challenges
- Many countries represented here today are using similar strategies:
    - Forming "Alianzas"
    - Involving the local private sector
    - Working and partnering with the media, community organizations, private sector, and communication professions
    - Using market research

Some Examples

- Brazil's "Parceria Contra Drogas" is one of Brazil's top 20 advertisers
- Argentina's "Consejo Publicitario Argentino" is one of the country's top 5 advertisers
- Puerto Rico's "Alianza para un Puerto Rico Sin Drogas" is one of Puerto Rico's top 5 advertisers
- Venezuela's "Alianza para una Venezuela Sin Drogas" is one of the country's top 5 advertisers
- New "Alianzas" have just been formed in Uruguay and Peru

Good ideas are already crossing borders

Venezuela: parenting skills "animals" spot

Uruguay: parental efficacy "missed opportunity" spot

U.S.:   parental efficacy "breakfast" spot

U.S. Approach

- Research-based campaign (Campaign Expert Design Panel, etc.)
- Studied other social marketing campaigns (seat belts, underage drinking, anti-tobacco, healthier living campaigns)
- Focus on "teens" (11 to 13), then teens and adults
- Focus on gateway drugs (marijuana and inhalants)
- Alcohol and tobacco included in pro bono match, not in paid media campaign
- Multi-pronged strategy; fully integrated campaign ads, school programs, television programming, interactive, media outreach, partnerships with youth and parent-serving organizations
- Rigorously evaluate what works

Set realistic goals:

- Educate and enable America's youth to reject illegal drugs
- Prevent youth from initiating use of drugs, especially marijuana and inhalants
- Convince occasional users of these and other drugs to stop using drugs

Set measurable results:

- By 2002, reduce past-month use of illegal drugs and alcohol among youth by 20% versus 1996
- By 2007, reduce past-month use by 50% versus 1996
- By 2002, increase average age of first time drug use by 12 months versus 1996
- By 2007, increase average first-time use by 36 months versus 1996

What Makes This Campaign Unique?

- Most extensive integrated marketing and public health communications campaign ever undertaken
- Multiple audiences reached where they live, work and play (from the internet to movies, from the school classroom to the office cafeteria, from television to sports stadiums, from pediatricians to work sites)
- Culturally relevant messages in 11 languages
- "Surround approach" to media (360 degrees)
- Influencing the total message environment
- Example: programming featuring anti-drug messages

Influencing messages in all parts of youth environment (not just ads)
Ad message platforms "flighted" across every media vehicle:

Youth: "Normative Education"
              "Positive Consequences"
              "Resistance Skills"
              "Negative Consequences"

Adults: "Parent Efficacy"
              "Parenting Skills"
              "Perceptions of Harm"
              "Your Child at Risk"

What Messages Are Likely To Work Best?

Consumer insight driven
Scientifically based

Example: for Spanish-speaking youth and adults certain values are especially important:

"familismo"   - the importance of family

"dignidad"   - individual self worth

"respeto"   - the value of rituals and ceremonies which guide behaviors

"caridad"   - a priority for helping other

Spanish-speaking people in need

We can leverage these values in our communications by: Placing emphasis on respect for family and discouraging behaviors which harm or threaten family unity. Developing gender-specific advertising which recognizes different vulnerabilities of girls and boys Developing messages based on research on the attitudes and perception of each target audience.

Reflecting ethnic pride and traditional Hispanic cultural values. (High levels of cultural traditionalism have been found to correlate with reduced likelihood of drug use) Positive role modeling regarding resistance skills, personal skills and peer support.

Examples: Puerto Rico: "Basketball" spot
             Puerto Rico: "Boxer" spot

Who Do We Partner With To Be Successful?

<u>Target Audience Specialists</u>: For kids, teens, adults and each ethnic group

<u>Behavior Change Experts</u>: The academic foundation of the campaign
National Institute Drug Abuse (NIDA)

<u>The Ad Council</u>: 85% of pro-bono match is Ad Council advertising with drug-related themes
Partnership for a Drug-Free America hugely successful model

Media Owners:

- All major TV networks and every media owner in radio, print, internet, out of home media
- Entertainment Industry
- Producers, network executives, writers, celebrities (who donate their time)
- Community Anti-Drug Coalitions of America (CADCA)
- Faith Communities: *e.g.* National Council of Black Churches
- Grassroots Organizations: *e.g.* YMCA, etc.
- Expert Contractors: *e.g.* Fleishman-Hillard
- Expert Evaluation: National Institute on Drug Abuse, Westat, Annenberg School of Communication

How Do We Measure and Sustain Success?

- Learning from other countries
- Constant evolution of the campaign (BCEP, Target Audience Specialists)
- Awareness and attitude tracking 365 days per year
- Westat Behavioral Outcomes Evaluation over 5 years
  Communications mapping (which media vehicle is most effective in communicating each message)

3 Lessons Learned:

- The campaign is working (awareness is up and anti-drug attitudes are strengthening)
- The U.S. campaign will be stronger if we can learn more about your campaigns and your success stories
- The U.S. still hasn't learned what time lunch and dinner should be eaten!

Thank you and I wish you
great success with your campaigns.

"Alianza. La Anti Drogas"

VI: Current and Future Trends in Drug Trafficking

Ronald K. Noble, Secretary General ICPO-Interpol – Nominee, United States

Biography

Ronald K. Noble is a Professor of Law at the New York University School of Law and is Secretary General ICOP-Interpol Nominee. His areas of specialization include: federal criminal law, evidence, gun control and money laundering. He currently serves as a member of Interpol's 12 member Executive Committee and recently served as President of the Financial Action Task Force -- a 26 country member group formed by the G-7 in 1989 to fight money laundering. Mr. Noble served as Under Secretary for Enforcement for the Department of the Treasury from 1994-1996. In that capacity he oversaw four of the eight largest federal law enforcement agencies in the United States: The Secret Service, the Customs Service, the Bureau of Alcohol, Tobacco and Firearms, and the Criminal Investigation Division of the Internal Revenue Service. Mr. Noble served as Deputy Assistant Attorney General and Special Counsel in the Criminal Division of the Department of Justice from 1988 until 1989, following a four-year term as Assistant United States Attorney for the Eastern District of Pennsylvania. Mr. Noble received a J.D. from Stanford Law School and a B.A. in Economics and Business Administration from the University of New Hampshire. Mr. Noble was born in Fort Dix, New Jersey.

A Truly Global Anti-Drug Strategy

As I read over the program and as look out across the room, I recognize that many of you devote and have devoted most of your professional lives to analyzing the question of what are the appropriate ingredients and mix of ingredients for an effective, fair and safe anti-drug strategy. You are the experts! The amount of knowledge and experience represented here today is indeed overwhelming.

So, what I hope to do is to give you the mixed perspective of a former prosecutor, a former Chief Law Enforcement Officer who oversaw the U.S. Customs Service which attempts to protect the U.S. borders from illegal drug trafficking and which investigates smuggling. I also will draw on my experience as the former President of the Financial Action Task Force which is a 26-member country group established in 1989 by the G-7 to fight money laundering stemming from drug trafficking.

Finally, over the last year in connection with my campaign to become Interpol's next Secretary General, I traveled to 18 countries on six continents. In each of those countries the issue of illegal drug trafficking and consumption was an issue of great importance to police, customs and law enforcement officials and immediately after this conference I will fly to Seoul Korea for Interpol's 1999 General Assembly Session where the representatives of Interpol's 177 Member States police agencies will gather. The issue of combating drug trafficking will also be high on Interpol's agenda.

Based on my professional experience and my travel over the last several years, my long held view of what lies over the drug trafficking horizon as we approach the next millennium was greatly reinforced. First, drug trafficking is a business, albeit an illegal one, which enjoys the many benefits of businesses operating during a time of rapid technological expansion. Drug traffickers have and continue to adapt their trafficking techniques and patterns. They monitor and react to the pressures our governments bring to bear on their business. They monitor and react to the changing desires of their customers. They improve old drugs; they trademark various brands and they bring new products to the market place. Drug traffickers throughout the world have greater access to supplies, equipment and revenue than the police agencies, customs services, police agencies and prosecutors fighting them. And, they are not bound by regulatory, constitutional or legal constraints.

I speak now primarily to law enforcement officials and government officials, but I believe what I say applies to all of us. As I read through the following list, think about whether your institutions use the following items, whether all of these items have been around forever or whether some are new; and finally, whether drug trafficking organizations have more or less access to these items than your institutions:

Communication: Cell phones
Pagers
Computers
Internet
Encoded Message Capability
Wire transfers
Fax Machines
Radios
Government Postal Service
Private Courier Services

Transportation:	Commercial airlines
	Trains
	Buses
	Private jets
	Freighters
	High Speed Boats
	Tunnels
	Tractor Trailers
	Trucks
	Cars

Personnel:	Businessman
	Chemists
	Craftsmen
	Managers
	Security Forces
	Pilots
	Drivers
	Couriers
	Bankers
	High-risk taking couriers
	Desperate couriers

Sophisticated Marketing Techniques:	Old products to improved products
	Trendy products
	Specialized Products
	Market Segmentation
	Product Differentiation

| **Governmental Support:** | Corrupt Public Officials |

The above list of items is not a comprehensive list. I use it to remind myself of how many points of contact there are between drug trafficking organizations and our societies. I also use it to remind myself of how great our challenge is. While some of the characteristics of drug trafficking have been around since the beginning of time, such as high-risk taking couriers and varieties of transportation vehicles and concealment techniques, other forms are of only of recent making. Consequently, the two constant characteristics of the drug business is that it is a business; and that the drug business is both ever changing and constant at the same time.

Why? Because since the memory of man or woman runneth not to the contrary, human beings have desired mind -altering drugs and over time societies have responded by outlawing many of these drugs. So, like any business as long as there is a demand for illegal drugs, individuals or criminal groups will attempt to find ways to supply people with these illegal drugs for profit. To achieve this end, criminal groups have over time used all of the tools and resources at their disposal (both old and modern). We should expect this trend to continue in the future. Also, not all criminal groups use the same business philosophy or marketing strategy. They do not use the "one glove fits all approach." Some groups make profit by generating a high-quality illegal product and marketing it just right to increase profits while other criminal groups prefer to use extortion, murder, violence intimidation and corruption to keep- or expand the market share of their illegal product.

Similarly the specific approach of one country may not be easily adaptable to another country.

Employing the business model approach to analyze drug trafficking may seem like too sterile an approach to take to this problem. But, I believe that many drug traffickers are not just cold-blooded killers; they are cold-blooded businessmen and women in the business of marketing dangerous products that always have been and always will be in demand in some form or another.

So, the emerging trend that I see for the next century is: Not just more of the same, but more of the same being executed more quickly and efficiently than at the turn of the last century for sure, but even more quickly and efficiently than 10 or even 5 years ago.

If you agree that this is true, does it mean that our struggle is hopeless? I say not only "no", but absolutely not. There is room for hope; there is a need for one resolve; and there is a requirement for our coordination efforts.

If drug traffickers are getting smarter, are remaining flexible and are determined to succeed at all costs, then so must societies, citizens, governments, police agencies, customs services and politicians.

How? Here I address law enforcement officials in particular, but others as well. We must be careful how we measure the problem and how we measure progress. We must direct our limited resources appropriately. We also must ensure that in our efforts to tackle this problem, we do not sacrifice the integrity of our institutions, the human rights of our citizens, and the fair application of the criminal law. Finally, we must resist the temptation to continue to view the drug trafficking problem as principally a law enforcement and criminal law problem.

This is what my professional experience and what my work with those tasked with fighting the problem tells me. Thus, today, rather than try to tell you about current and future trends of the drug traffickers, which will have changed again before I conclude my remarks, I would like to discuss with you principles that we as policy makers should consider and debate in our common cause against this menace to our peoples.

Why do I feel so strongly about proposing new trends for policy makers rather than reviewing trends of drug traffickers? I've already alluded to it. The time lag between reports on changing trends and implementing new policies to address changing trends of trafficking patterns is too great. For example, next week Interpol will review in detail recent trends in drug trafficking patterns. I have an advance copy of Interpol's Report on Illicit Drug Trafficking that will be presented at next week's 1999 General Assembly in Seoul, Korea. The supporting documentation and the report itself focus on the 1998 calendar year. Think about it: Activity back in 1998 will be the basis for police officers deciding how to fight crime in 2000. I don't want to fall into that trap. I prefer to tell you about the report, encourage you to read it in the privacy of your office or home and to use my time to talk about new approaches for us to consider implementing.

Let me briefly outline them for you now:

First, I would like to talk about our choices of success measures and the weight we attach to these measures. Second, I wish to emphasize the importance of devoting the necessary resources to hiring, training, paying and equipping our government, police and customs officials, and how failing to pay the appropriate amount of attention to any one of these elements will not only harm our common goal, but it will expose our societies to the risk of having our civil servants become ripe targets for corruption. Third, it will be no surprise that as a former Under Secretary of U.S. Department of the Treasury, I believe that we must give high priority to the money side of the drug business. Fourth and finally, law enforcement must open its doors to all elements of the private sector and civil society to gain allies in our common struggle.

Measures of Success -

It is perhaps inevitable that ever since we began referring to our efforts against the drug problem as a war, we began measuring successes like warriors. Seizure statistics and arrests are comparable to body counts. While -the United States has an outstanding former General as its anti-drug leader, Barry McCaffrey, he knows all to well that such measures often give a false sense of security. While using statistics is necessary, General McCaffrey has demonstrated- during a recent trip to Europe the kind of statistics that are helpful.

For example, General McCaffrey disclosed that drug use in the United States has dropped by 50% over the last two decades. Cocaine use is down 70%. Drug use among American adolescents age 12-17 went down 13% last year. These statistics are valuable. Statistics about average price changes and purity levels are also valuable.

But, the statistic that I see used much too casually and viewed too uncritically is the seizure statistic. Some might say that it is provocative for the Secretary General Nominee of Interpol - the world's largest police organization-to question the use of seizure statistics to measure the drug problem. But if we are to improve our anti-drug effort, we must be candid.

Seizures

In every country in which I met with and discussed the drug trafficking problem with police officers, customs officials and government officials, seizures were used to explain the extent of the problem or the effectiveness of the fight. Why? What do we learn of value from the amount of a seizure? Do cocaine seizures in the U.S. account for the 70% reduction in cocaine use? What percentage of cocaine is believed to be in use? What percentage is believed to have been seized. Seizure numbers must be used to tell us something more than the weight or number of seizures. Why?

Two Quick Examples:

1. Seizure numbers can go up because we are finding more of it, but the rate of consumption could have remained unchanged.

2. Seizure numbers can go up because the amount of trafficking is increasing but our seizure percentage is simply a constant.

Let me put it another way. Years ago, the DEA and other national drug police began to focus on dismantling complex trafficking organizations. During this changed philosophy, the number of arrests went down but the quality of arrests went up. However, convincing politicians and budget folks of this important distinction and change in our measures was not easy.

Don't get me wrong, there is valuable information one can glean from seizures. In my view valuable information comes not from the weight or number of seizures, but from the how, where, and type of seizures.

Let me use cocaine and some of the information gleaned from Interpol's 1998 drug trafficking trend report to help make my point of how seizures can help us.

Europe:

Seizures can tell us about trafficking methods and patterns. For example, in Eastern Europe during 1998, the traffickers were using much smaller vehicles to ship smaller loads of cocaine; false-sided travel bags and suitcases were used to complement the use of smaller vehicles. Armed with this information, customs officers and border guards can appropriately direct their efforts.

Of course human couriers continue to be used by drug traffickers, except that in Eastern Europe the nationalities of couriers included more couriers from the end point Eastern European countries. This is helpful to customs officials and border guards, but it also helpful to civil liberty advocates and people of color who may suffer discrimination when crossing borders because of profiling techniques. If reports say that drug traffickers are using European couriers and not only African couriers, then the Customs and Border officials conducting searches based on negative stereotypes will be forced to change their conduct when deciding whom to search.

Caribbean:

Seizures also tell us what common sense tells us. The more pressure governments bring to bear on one entry point, then the more likely it is that traffickers will quickly adjust their delivery routes. For that reason, 1998 saw an increase of trafficking occurring in the Caribbean as a result of the beefing up of the effort to reduce smuggling along the Southwest Border of the U.S. Seizures permitted us to interview traffickers and to learn from them that a shift from the southwest to the southeast of the U.S. had occurred.

Africa:

Seizures in South Africa reveal that it is becoming an important transshipment point of cocaine originating in South America and destined for Europe. Here again, the seizures led to arrests, which led to getting defendants to cooperate, which led to valuable intelligence information.

So, I humbly submit. The naked fact that x pounds or tons of cocaine were seized tells us very little of value as we decide how to formulate our policies. Just as in war, body counts are not a measure of progress; so seizure counts should not be a measure of success or failure. Moreover, if we pick the wrong measures such as uncritically assessed seizures, we will waste scarce resources in areas that really do not make a difference. So, resist the temptation to feel good or bad about your policies based on naked seizure statistics.

The Quality of Our Police Forces, their Investigative Resources and Corruption -

I recently participated in the Bi-annual International Anti-Corruption Conference sponsored by Transparency International. It was widely attended by both governmental and private sector representatives. Several heads of sate, heads of private industry, and heads of non-profits spoke. I was honored to speak after the Vice President of Colombia. During my remarks, I asked for a showing of hands from among the 1400 or so attendees to see how many police officials were in attendance. Only a few individuals raised their hands, and only 3 heads of police agencies from throughout the world were in attendance.

Why is this important? The police are an insular community. They need constant exposure to the private sector, civil society and other professionals so as to help them discharge their mission. For example, police have discretion and power to enforce or not enforce the law. Thus, they are at great risk of becoming targets for corruption by drug traffickers. The people we hire, the way in which we train them and the amount we pay them and the environment or culture in which we place them will determine in part how vulnerable they are to corruption. Right?

So, we should get our police officers out among the world's community and we should dedicate the appropriate resources at the front end to hiring the right kind of people; to training them; to policing them; and to paying them so as to reduce the risk of corruption.

Once we have highly trained and supervised, honest, ethical, and properly paid police officers, then good policies have a chance of succeeding. But, only then.

On the practical side, why can't the world's wealthiest countries commit themselves to funding the establishment of state of the art communication centers for police and customs services throughout the world to inter-communicate with one another, and those in a civil society. Imagine a world where a customs official or police officer in each country would have access to information about ways in which drug smuggling is occurring as it's occurring. So, if a seizure is made at a port of entry in Turkey where traffickers were using a certain smuggling method, that information could be entered into a database and any country could retrieve and download the relevant information and distribute it to its personnel as needed. If smugglers are using a particular secret compartment in one part of the world, it is likely that they are using it in another part of the world as well. For police and customs officials relevant and timely intelligence is an invaluable tool.

For the police and customs officials, they need to move away from worrying about holding too closely what intelligence they are finding. Each time traffickers learn that police are on to a technique they are using for smuggling, they must change the technique. Constant change is costly and risky.

Let's invest in our people in the public sector like the private industry invests in people in the private sector. We have an interest in doing this whether we are the biggest demand country or supply country. For example, Colombia reportedly produces 80 percent of the world's cocaine and about two-thirds of the heroin-consumed in the United States. It thus makes sense for both Colombia and the U.S. to coordinate their efforts and to share information about smuggling methods. And, it's appropriate for the U.S. to aid Colombia financially and for Colombia to ensure that the money is wisely invested and targeted. This kind of collaboration needs to be encouraged worldwide.

Money & Drugs -

The leaders of the world drug trafficking organizations are not in the business of supplying drugs as their ultimate goal. They are in the money business. They are trying to create wealth just as any business attempts to make profits. Indeed, the smart leaders of these organizations stay well away from the activity of drug trafficking. If we focus all of our energy on those who process, transport and sell drugs we will make lots of arrests, we will make lots of seizures but we will have little impact on the people at the top of the organizations. They can stay away from the drug trafficking activity, but they will never stray far from their profits. As in any business, they need access to the world's financial system and it is there that we must focus our energy. Unfortunately, we have few investigators who have the education, training or resources to follow the financial trail to the people who count the most. The effort to address money laundering is not simply to seize the proceeds of crime, but to link the proceeds with organizers at the top of the drug trafficking organizations. Colombia has had some recent success in Operation Millennium, which resulted in the arrest of Jorge Ochoa. Indeed, the efforts at dismantling the Medellin and Cali cartels were in no small measure the result of efforts at disrupting their financial empires.

But, the Ministries of Interior and Justice need help from the Ministries of Finance and from Regulatory institutions to ensure that financial data is both kept and made accessible to law enforcement and to ensure that drug traffickers' funds are at risk when placed in financial institutions.

Expanding Law Enforcement's Allies -

It is key that we break down the barriers that often separate law enforcement from the private sector and the communities they serve. The drug problem requires a reaching out to all elements of society. This is not simply a law enforcement matter. General McCaffrey has devoted much of his time to this aspect and deserves great credit. His leadership on the drug testing issue for athletes and the public advertising campaigns are just two examples. We in law enforcement must lead but we also must listen. We can't let our societies simply assume that we are in charge and thus they can go on with their work. Countries that create national drug offices cannot let the great politicians, other agencies and the public see that as the solution and proceed as if they had no further role. In addition, we in law enforcement must be comfortable in taking criticism and avoid circling the wagons, if I may use an old western movie analogy. If we want to determine how dirty money flows, for example, we will have to ask the bankers for help. We must also engage the academic world, if we are to develop the best measures of progress. Economist as well as criminologist, for example, can be of great aid. To develop anti-corruption programs, we will need help from the business community and on and on.

Conclusions -

We have a great challenge in an important cause. We should approach our duties with great humility. We cannot speak of winning or losing. This is a struggle that we will be engaged in as long as there is a demand for drugs. We must be honest with ourselves and our citizens that while progress is achievable, victory cannot be honestly defined as 100% elimination of the problem. However, we can try to take the great wealth out of the drug trafficking business and that will reduce the problem of corruption. We can only do this by ensuring that we have the right measures to determine progress and that all the elements of our society are engaged in this cause. Thank you very much.

VII: Law Enforcement Strategies for the Future

Walter Maierovitch, Secretary, National Antidrug Secretariat, (SENAD), Brazil

Biography

Walter Maierovitch was appointed by President Cardoso in November 1998 as the first head of the National Antidurg Secretariat, which is directly linked to the office of the President. During his three decades as a career judge, he acquired extensive expertise in the area of transnational crime. His personal commitment in that struggle, particularly in anti-mafia campaigns in close cooperation with Italian magistrates, resulted in national and international recognition.

**OFFICE OF THE PRESIDENT
INSTITUTIONAL SECURITY OFFICE
NATIONAL ANTIDRUG SECRETARIAT**

GOVERNO FEDERAL

NATIONAL ANTIDRUG SECRETARIAT

LAW ENFORCEMENT STRATEGIES FOR THE FUTURE

PRELIMINARY THOUGHTS

Transnational Crime:

Illicit and abused drugs represent the main source of profits:

✔ they account between 3 and 5% of the world's Gross Domestic Product;

✔ very high social cost: in some countries it represents 4% of the GDP.

World Conference on Transnational Crime:
From November 21 -.23, 1994 NAPLES

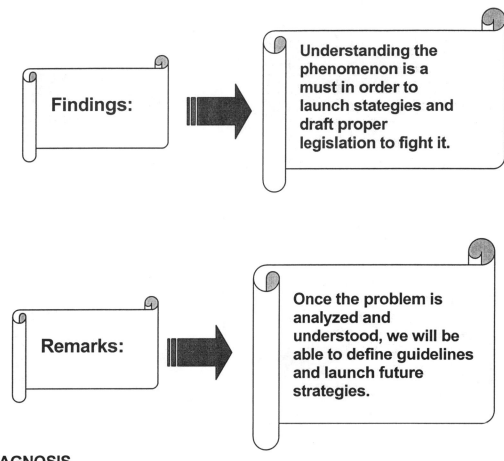

Findings: ➔ Understanding the phenomenon is a must in order to launch stategies and draft proper legislation to fight it.

Remarks: ➔ Once the problem is analyzed and understood, we will be able to define guidelines and launch future strategies.

DIAGNOSIS

✔ increase in the supply and demand of drugs;

✔ the power of corruption;

✔ social and territorial control;

✔ States with dependent economies;

✔ annhilation of the democratic State;

✔ commitment to individual freedoms and rights;

✔ power system and search for easy profit;

Intermediation:

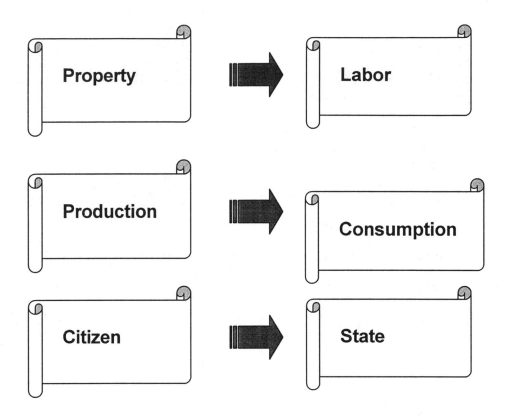

*"Transnational organizations represent the
most serious danger to civil society in our time."*

- Louis Freeh

THE FUTURE

✓ rule of law
✓ international cooperation.
✓ aiming at the economy of Organized Crime.

⇒ bank control enforcement;

⇒ immediate sale by auction of assets seized from drug traffickers, carried out by a Judge and a preventive trial;

⇒ establishment of an international financial control body, composed of high ranking officials responsible for coordinatinating and carrying out law enforcement measures;

⇒ control of electronic fund transfers: transfer of monies;

⇒ trends in market "pathology": attraction of investments;

⇒ tax havens = stock markets = art dealers markets, etc...

⇒ International Court of Justice to prosecute international drug dealers;

⇒ Trusteeship sales = control = mechanism to facilitate the use of assets.

LAW ENFORCEMENT AND CRIMINAL STATUTES

✓ encouragement of the use of informants and means of rewarding them;
✓ infiltration of criminal organizations;
✓ acceptance of *in absentia* trial;
✓ strict discipline incarceration;
✓ support for task forces in the Americas;
✓ covert international operations;
✓ expedite extradictions of nationals;
✓ simplified rogatory letters;
✓ international system of witness protection and experts.

ADMINISTRATIVE RULES

✓ **Drug tests for high ranking officials and police officers;**

✓ **control of chemical precursors;**

✓ **control of pharmaceutical drugs;**

✓ **monitoring by satellite and exchange of reports;**

✓ **multilateral certification procedures;**

✓ **police academies = professional training courses with international support and evaluation;**

✓ **basic rules for operations carried out by law enforcement bodies = police; intelligence; The Judiciary; Antidrug National Secretariats.**

FINAL REMARKS

For future strategies, we must remember:

"In democracies, the drug trade flourishes only when it can divide the population and corrupt institutions"

- General BARRY R. McCAFFREY

VII: Law Enforcement Strategies for the Future

Brigadier Joseph L. Theodore, Minister of National Security, Trinidad and Tobago

Biography

Brigadier Joseph L. Theodore serves as Minister of National Security for Trinidad & Tobago. He formerly served as Chief of Defense Staff, retiring at the rank of Brigadier in 1991. Theodore is a graduate of the Royal Military Academy and the Army Staff College in Camberely, United Kingdom. He was appointed a Senator and Minister of National Security in 1995. He holds responsibility for Defense and Law Enforcement and National Emergency Management and serves as Chairman of the Defense Board and as a member of its National Security Council. He is also the representative of Trinidad & Tobago on its Council of Ministers of the CFATF and the CARICOM Inter-Governmental Task Force on Drugs.

Law Enforcement Strategies for the Future

As we discuss law enforcement strategies for the future, it is important to consider in broad terms, what nature future law enforcement challenges are likely to take. We face a serious criminal phenomenon that possesses some basic features, which clearly would endure into the next millennium.

One such feature is the absence of borders. Drug trafficking is an increasingly borderless crime. No doubt, the criminals have been ahead of us in this respect. Internationalization and globalization, have been practical features of this criminal activity, long before we were able to move ahead with the establishment of legal and enforcement systems that facilitated cross-border enforcement co-operation. Indeed, the criminals were not inhibited by traditional notions of sovereignty; mutual support and co-operation have always been key features.

Another characteristic of this phenomenon is that the drug trade is a highly lucrative big business. We must accept therefore, that it will be well nigh impossible to pressure entrepreneurs into abandoning this lucrative industry. We have already witnessed the shift from product to product - cocaine to heroin to synthetic drugs etc. - and the exploitation of global trade facilitation mechanisms in the process of these activities. Not the least of these is the use by traffickers of rapidly advancing technology.

Yet another feature in the evolution, is the advances in money laundering techniques, to the point where large investments of criminal money have been used to capitalize legitimate commercial activity.

All of this means that the profile and characteristics of law enforcement for the future, must change commensurately. Globalization establishes the need for interdependence as a key requirement in successful counter strategies. More than ever, the future will require increased operational collaboration based on even further advances in enabling legal frameworks. These must enable more rapid exchange of information and intelligence and faster mobilization of collective law enforcement resources across borders. The availability of technology in law enforcement tools and the training of operatives in the use of technology, must become a standard feature.

Drug trafficking is here for the long term. It has also influenced the nature of traditional crime and spawned new crimes. We therefore need to consider whether the emphasis -on specialized units focusing on drug trafficking investigations, need to be complemented by the balanced upgrading of the capabilities of the wider law enforcement community. It is this community which is faced with tackling the increasing sophistication in the commission of traditional crimes enhanced by drug trafficking. Indeed, the new strategies must recognize the inter dependence between drug trafficking and traditional criminal activities. Particularly in small jurisdictions, specialized units are established within national police organizations, Many of the drug seizures and drug arrests are effected by officers and units outside of the specialized units. This makes the case for the balanced upgrading of the organization in general. Moreover, in these situations, the perceived over emphasis on equipping and training specialized units, sometimes acts against inclusiveness and the commitment of the total organization to address the problem.

The multi-faceted nature of the threat and the need for community mobilization against it requires that law enforcement engage and participate with the wider society in its efforts. This requires specific strategies for public communication and public mobilization. The model of community policing will perhaps need to be expanded to embrace these wider concepts.

Another issue is that of corruption. Nothing is more debilitating to law enforcement efforts than corruption within the ranks. There is no evidence that our efforts and strategies to date have resulted in a significant reduction in the levels of corruption within the ranks of law enforcement. We need therefore, to re-examine these measures. We clearly need to establish and enhance Internal Investigation Units, but the situation suggests that we would do well to consider a wider regime of measures to combat corruption.

If we may come back to the issue of inter dependence among nations, I should like to refer to the spirit of the Multilateral Evaluation Mechanism (MEM) and the outstanding progress that it has made so far. One of the basic intentions of this evaluation mechanism is to promote mutual support. As we thrive for improvement in law enforcement, it may be useful for us to consider agreeing upon a minimum set of measures for enforcement organizations and for the initiation of a mutual evaluation process among law enforcement organizations, with a view to identifying weaknesses and areas for mutual support. This has certainly worked well in the Caribbean region at the level of the Caribbean Financial Action Task Force (CFATF) against the problem of money laundering.

At present there are twenty-five (25) Caribbean Basin States who have signed the Memorandum of Understanding (MOU) establishing the Caribbean Financial Action Task Force (CFATF). In the first round of mutual evaluation, nineteen (19) Member States have already undergone evaluation. The second round of evaluations is due to commence in 2001. This evaluation program has enabled Member States to benefit from a focused regional program designed to improve the capability of the region to combat the problem of money laundering.

In summary therefore, as we consider law enforcement strategies for the future, the following areas stand out as essential for effective law enforcement:

Co-operation –

This will include:
- Domestic inter-agency co-operation.
- Cross border co-operation among agencies.
- Co-operation with the public in general.
- The use of technology.
- Training to satisfy the new profile for law enforcement.
- Mutual Evaluation among law enforcement services.

VIII: Social and Economic Costs of Drugs

Eduardo Amadeo, Secretary, National Anti-Drug Secretariat, (SEDRONAR), Argentina

Biography

Eduardo Pablo Amadeo is a trained enconomist who serves as Secretary of State for Antidrug Affairs. Amadeo received an undergraduate degree in Economics from the Catholic University of Argentina in 1970 and a graduate degree in Scientific and Technological Policy from Sussex University, Great Britain in 1972. He has also served as a resident scholar at the Woodrow Wilson Center in Washington. Dr. Amadeo has held numerous teaching positions, including as Professor of Economic Policy at the University of Buenos Aires School of Law and Social Sciences and as Professor of Social Policy of the Latin-American University for Social Sciences. Amadeo served as President of the Buenos Aires Provincial Bank from 1987-1991. He was formerly a Member of the Parliament and Chairman of the Education Committee from 1991-1994. Dr. Amadeo served as Minister of Social Development from 1994-1998.

National Anti-Drug Secretariat (SEDRONAR)

THE COSTS OF DRUGS
The Social, Economic, and Political

WHY MEASURE?

♦ Science - Ideology - decisions

♦ Integral Measuring as a tool for systemic integration of governmental decisions (assigning resources - impact)

♦ Raise Social Consciousness

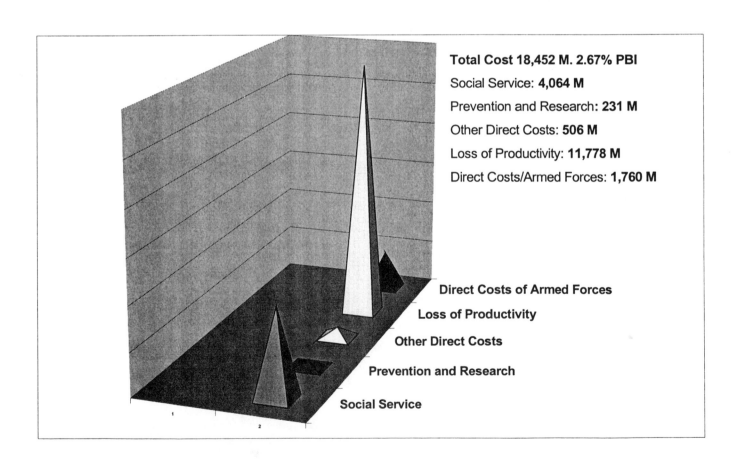

Total Cost 18,452 M. 2.67% PBI

Social Service: **4,064 M**

Prevention and Research: **231 M**

Other Direct Costs: **506 M**

Loss of Productivity: **11,778 M**

Direct Costs/Armed Forces: **1,760 M**

Direct Costs of Armed Forces
Loss of Productivity
Other Direct Costs
Prevention and Research
Social Service

UNDERSTAND INTEGRALLY

◆ Epidemiological Data
◆ Causes
◆ Cultural and Social Attitudes
◆ Costs
◆ Results

IMPACT OF DRUG AND ALCOHOL USE IN THE U.S.A.

◆ 45% Family
◆ 39% Government
◆ 10% Insurance
◆ 6% Victims

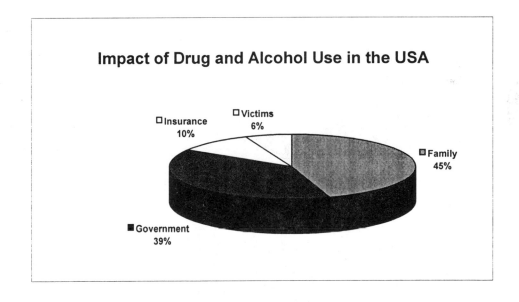

VIII: Social and Economic Costs of Drugs

Jacques LeCavalier, Chief Executive Officer Canadian Centre on Substance Abuse (CCSA), Canada

Biography

Jacques LeCavalier is the Chief Executive Officer of the Canadian Center on Substance Abuse (CCSA). This organization was created by an Act of Parliament in 1988 to provide a national focus for substance abuse issues in Canada. Prior to joining CCSA, he set up Canada's Drug Strategy Secretariat (CDSS) and made important contributions to the renewal of the Strategy in 1992. Mr. LeCavalier has served on many UN/WHO/G7 expert groups and led the Canadian delegation to the UN Commission on Narcotic Drugs for many years. In the 80's he was Director of the Bureau of Dangerous Drugs, responsible for drug control legislation and for controlling the movement and use of psychoactive pharmaceuticals. Mr. LeCavalier is a pharmacist with public administration training.

CCSA · CCLAT

Drug Abuse Cost Estimates
A blueprint for better decision support

Drug control decision-making

- Everyone has a "pet" solution

- In fact, we know very little about what works and what doesn't

- Decisions made on "intuition" in successive episodes of panic and indifference

- Decisions are seldom evaluated for impact

- Compelling need for evidence-based model

- Cost matters

Key policy questions

- What are the costs of drug abuse to society?

- What portion of these costs is realistically avoidable?

- What and where should we invest to avoid these costs?

- What is our return on investment over time?

Costs to society

- What costs to include?

- Costs to whom?

- Data availability

- Methodology gaps

- Addressing intangibles

- Impact of "shadow" economy

- Policy utility

Estimating avoidable costs

◆ Purpose

⇒ Setting achievable objectives with realistic targets

◆ Issues to be tackled

⇒ Some costs are unavoidable

⇒ Choosing realistic counterfactual scenarios

⇒ Focusing on patterns of use and consequences

⇒ Methodology gaps

What and where to invest?

◆ Purpose

⇒ Setting appropriate investment/intervention levels and optimal mix

◆ Issues to be tackled

⇒ Methodology gaps:

- Cost/benefit, cost/effectiveness, cost/utility techniques as applied to the illicit drug scene

What return on investment?

◆ Purpose

⇒ Adapt/adjust strategies, policies and programs

◆ Issues to be tackled

⇒ establishing an appropriate time frame

⇒ Setting specific outcome indicators and performance measures at the onset

⇒ making complementary qualitative assessments in attributing cost reductions to policies

Where are we today?

- We have barely started!
- International Guidelines for cost estimation
  - ⇒ Implemented in several countries
  - ⇒ Being tested and adapted in different settings
- Some more advanced work conducted for specific interventions - i.e. treatment
- Worldwide interest in cost estimation

Next steps: development and cooperation

- Addressing methodology gaps related to crime costs, misuse of pharmaceuticals, shadow economies and lost productivity
- Moving to other stages of economic analysis with greater policy utility
- Enhancing cooperation
  - ⇒ Multi-disciplinary: economists, policy advisors, researchers, drug control specialists, police, etc.
  - ⇒ Multi-lateral: economy of scale, comparability

Conclusion

- Compelling need for evidence-based model of decision-making which addresses costs
- Answers to the 4 key questions will narrow the range of uncertainty in policy making
- Some critical success factors:
  - ⇒ Political leadership and long-term commitment to the development, testing and adaptation of better tools
  - ⇒ A mindset conducive to sharing and partnerships

VIII: Social and Economic Costs of Drugs

Claudio Molina, Counselor, National Drug Control Agency, (CONACE), Chile

Biography

Dr. Claudio Molina is coordinator of the National Council for Narcotics Control of Chile and a Member of the team which developed the national drug information system in Chile (this included design of three national studies and a map of vulnerability). The National Council prepares annual reports on the drug problem in Chile. Dr. Molina also serves as Professor of Research Methodology for postgraduates and professors in service.

QUESTIONS REGARDING STUDIES ON THE SOCIAL
AND ECONOMIC COSTS OF DRUGS IN OUR COUNTRIES

1999 CONFERENCE OF REGIONAL DRUG POLICY LEADERS

In addition to cost study considerations related to policy matters and to methodology, there are other questions regarding implementation of these studies in our Latin American countries that need to be raised.

♦ Experience in implementing a cost study in your country

♦ Chilean proposal

Use of international guidelines: Are they relevant for developing countries?

International guidelines relate to the following issues:

- ♦ Definition and measure of abuse
- ♦ Causes
- ♦ Definition of costs
- ♦ Treatment for addiction
- ♦ Treatment of private costs
- ♦ Costs involved in social welfare
- ♦ Treatment of mortality and morbidity not related to employment
- ♦ Treatment of costs of prevention, research, training, and law enforcement

Which of these issues are important to our countries?
Are some more important than others, or are they all relevant?

There is no question that it is not only necessary to consider these international guidelines, but that it is essential if we are to develop descriptions and explanations that converge as closely as possible with reality.

Additional studies should be carried out to ensure a minimum amount of information on variables with cost implications, while the rest can be estimated. In any event, consideration should be given to all costs. Moreover, a rigorous methodology should be applied that includes methods and approaches involving both human and demographic considerations, along with a comparison of the results.

Do our countries have statistics to be used in these studies?

If they do exist, are these statistics accurate and reliable?

Do we have the political will and financing needed to generate the required information?

Do our countries have the technical capacity to generate the information required to conduct a drug cost study?

Developing countries should move towards more standardized information systems, adding technical and methodological value to all types of studies performed, either for the first time or in the broader context of international and national information systems, if they exist.

Are our countries developing drug information systems that are based, for instance, on national drug use studies, or on seizures, arrests, or other related statistics?

In this postindustrial age in which we live, information is the primary input and product.

Do studies of this sort enhance the visibility, image, institutionality, and credibility of national drug agencies?

Do they help strengthen interdisciplinary work teams?

Do they leave technical capacity installed for further studies?

It is important to take into account the commitment made by countries in the context of the MEM, which involves requests for information involving, among other things, matters related to the "existence of a system for estimating the human, social, and economic costs of the drug problem." OAS member states are expected to provide this information if they have it, generate it if they do not have it, or complete it if it is partial or relatively unreliable (MEM indicator 61).

Also included in the international guidelines are both the basic definitions and the instruments for obtaining data generated by CICAD/OAS groups of experts, and specifically the Data Bank Office and its Inter-American System of Standardized Drug Use Data (SIDUC).

What is the status of the countries with regard to information related to the 60 indicators from the first round of MEM indicators?

Should cost estimates include various fields and represent factors inherent in demand and control?

Examples of causes/variables that could be included (identification, selection, definition, and construction) in drug cost studies in our countries:

1. Direct costs of health care
1.1 Morbidity costs: general treatment and mental hospitals
1.2 Co-morbidity costs
1.3 Outpatient services
1.4 Home care
1.5 Treatment agencies
1.6 Medical fees for outpatient care and professional services
1.7 Prescription medicine
1.8 Other health care costs

2. Direct, job-related losses
2.1 Employee Health Care Programs and other health promotion programs at work.
2.2 Drug testing at work.

3. Direct administrative costs of transfer payments
3.1 Administrative costs of welfare and other programs
3.2 Administrative costs of employee remuneration
3.3 Other administrative costs

4. Direct costs for prevention and research and investigation
4.1 Research and investigation
4.2 Prevention programs, including fire and accident prevention
4.3 Costs of training physicians and nurses
4.4 Crime prevention costs

5. Direct law enforcement costs
5.1 Police
5.2 Courts
5.3 Correctional measures, including parole and probation
5.4 Customs and specific excise taxes

6. Other direct costs
6.1 Damage resulting from fire
6.2 Damage resulting from traffic accidents
6.3 Reduced property values in communities affected by drugs
6.4 Intangible costs

7. Indirect costs: losses in productivity
7.1 Reduced productivity due to morbidity
7.2 Losses in productivity due to mortality
7.3 Productivity losses due to crime and delinquency

Important considerations:

♦ It is not easy to decide which costs should be included in the study.

♦ The previous list is not exhaustive.

♦ When productivity losses resulting from drug-related illnesses are added to social welfare payments received by persons who are unable to work because of drug abuse, there is a dual cost involved.

♦ Police costs must be included, although not all police costs are associated with drug abuse.

♦ The inclusion of law enforcement and penal costs depends on various factors, which are not controversial and may all be included.

♦ The advisability of including certain law enforcement costs related to crimes against property and crimes of violence can be argued, but it is not easy to estimate the fraction to be attributed to those costs.

What should be done about cost items for which no information at all is available?

If they are not taken into account, then we are assuming that these items do not represent costs to the country, and if they are considered by making indirect estimates, these estimates may turn out to be unsatisfactory and relatively unreliable.

What drug costs studies are not:

♦ They are not avoidable cost studies.

♦ They are not cost-benefit analysis studies.

♦ They do not indicate the amount of money or the number of human years that could be realistically saved by an effective governmental and social program.

♦ They are not studies of the effect of drugs on the government budget, since they refer to all of society.

Availability of data, need for more research

If we analyze studies conducted on the subject, we see that there is a large number of variables, both related to prevention, treatment, and rehabilitation, and related to production and control of drug trafficking. Most countries do not have the information they need to perform cost studies, or at least not to perform studies in which the variables that represent costs to countries are defined. An effort should at least be made to perform the methodological exercise of designing complementary studies to produce information and, as an alternative, to design the mechanism for making the best possible estimate of the costs of variables that are part of the descriptive and explanatory model, when countries do not have the necessary information.

What are the keys to success in a cost study?

♦ Political support?
♦ Financial support?
♦ Installed technical capacity?
♦ Multi-professional and multi-sectoral teams?
♦ A multi-disciplinary approach to the problem?
♦ Shared responsibility in performing the work?
♦ Being open to new ideas and to learning from others' experience?

IX: Future Challenges to Drug Control Policy

Jorge Madrazo Cuellar, Attorney General, Mexico

Biography

Mr. Jorge Madrazo was appointed Attorney general of Mexico by President Zedillo on December 1996. From 1990 to 1996 Mr. Madrazo held several positions at the National Commission on Human Rights. He was appointed by the President of Mexico and Confirmed by the Mexican Senate as President of the Commission from 1993-1996. A professor of Constitutional Law, Mr. Madrazo held several positions at the Universidad Nacional Autonoma De Mexico (UNAM) between 1975 and 1990, including: Advisor t the Attorney General, Academic Secretary for the Institute of Legal Research, Coordinator of Social Sciences; and Dean of the Legal Research Institute. Mr. Madrazo was born in Mexico City in 1953. He obtained his Law degree at the UNAM, where he specialized in Constitution and Administrative law and pursued post-graduate master's and doctoral studies at the School of Law. He is the author of numerous essays and academic articles and has co-authored and edited several books on human rights and constitutional law in Mexico.

Reflections of the Drug Challenge in the Eve of the New Millennium. Note for our Memories.

The proximity of the new year, the new century and the new millennium as part of the social rituals of the artificial measure of our time is, emotionally but also rationally, a propitious opportunity to meditate collectively about the challenges encountered by mankind, as well as about the principles, values, methods and strategies that we shall utilize to face these challenges and to contribute, as far as our generations are incumbent, in the continuity of our Species.

I must express that the mere outline of the subject of this panel is a challenge in itself, not future but distressfully contemporary, at least for this person speaking, that increases proportionally to the point of being frankly dramatic in virtue of the fatality of the ten minutes allowed to fulfill this nearly impossible mission.

A first premise formulated by me as a manner of provocation, consists in visualizing the foreseeable challenges as a whole, as a unity, in order to conceive the solutions, to find the instruments and to design the strategies, with an idea of unity, examining each challenge in light of the others, thus working in a coordinated, organized and interactive manner.

If this premise is valid, then we would necessarily have to question about how the National States, the regional instances and the international organizations should be, in order to confront the challenges of a future that seems to have reached us and that, however, we are in a rush to joyfully celebrate in 55 days from now.

In my opinion, the beginning of the new millennium should be marked with the return to that humanism that was once envisioned in this agonizing century, losing the path for its attainment in some black hour of our existence. It is now time to place the human face as our port of destiny, as the axis of our aspirations, as the reason of all our efforts whether individual or collective.

Regarding the question of how to define a Humanist State, we would need not only to use all the time allowed to this speech, but the time of all speeches presented in all the conferences from today to at least the end of the century. To avoid this, and with all the risks implied therein, I dare to propose in a very pragmatic manner, the definition of the modern Humanist State as that capable of making real for its constituents, all those internationally declared and acknowledged Fundamental Rights of the human person, that is, the human rights of the so called three generations, starting from the fundamental freedom of the individual, to the rights of solidarity such as peace, development and the benefits that are common patrimony to mankind.

Therefore, a Humanist State requires of an economy at the service of human being; of a politics based in the same principle, or the scientific development and technology; education and culture; arts, communications, and Law, all of them with equal foundation and of course, of the humanist way of articulating the regional and international relations of the States.

Based on the aforementioned, it would necessarily be assumed that illegal drugs one of our most significant challenges. Therefore the regional and international policies of the States should be based and inspired in the same humanist principles that would regulate the global action of mankind and its collective forms of organizations. Having a humanist policy on illegal drugs is, in my opinion, the greatest of the drug related challenges imposed on the state organization, whether regional or international, as well as on the societies served by these structures. Thus, a humanist policy on illegal drugs is only the expression of a general State policy, based on social consensus and applied to this particular and specific challenge.

The next question should necessarily be: how a humanist policy on illicit drugs is characterized? How should this challenge be addressed while respecting and promoting the fundamental rights and liberties of the individual; his/her individual and collective prerogatives; his/her social and solidarity rights?

To answer this certainly complex question, it would be valid to first say what a humanist illicit drug policy is not. In this regard, allow me to make clear that the humanist policy does not mean legalization of drugs. To legalize drugs means to stop punishing those who produce, transport, distribute and trade it, induce to its consumption or even consume it, launder the financial dividends that these activities produce; this is certainly not humanizing the challenge.

The legalization of drugs presumes the cancellation of the challenge posed by its combat, but not the solution of the problems resulting from this activity. A legalization policy is based in theoretically or dogmatically converting a real problem into a non-existing one. It would be more like an act of illusion than an expression of true collective consciousness.

In order to be successful, the promoters of the legalization of drugs would have to demonstrate undoubtedly that illegal drugs do not damage or threaten the internationally acknowledged human rights, either individually nor collectively; that its consumption does not affect the autonomy of the individual's will; that therefore, it does not affect the individual's right to choose or free will; that it does not harm the public or individual health; that it is not a risk to the public safety; that it does not undermine the family unity; that it does not debilitate the economy; that it does not endanger the national security of the States; that it does not threaten the democratic institutions; that it does not deprive the strength of justice; that it does not generate individual or social discouragement or distress.

At least during the last two decades, we, that do not participate in the legalization current, have stated that illicit drugs do result in the aforementioned consequences. Then, why have we been unable to scientifically demonstrate it, in an irrefutable manner, so as to permit the consistent development of an extirpation strategy? Is it maybe that scientific progress, with the exactness that is inherent to it, is not so important so as to demonstrate that drugs do destroy?

Therefore, it seems that one of the priorities of a humanist antidrug policy would be to sufficiently demonstrate the harmful effects of drugs, to the end of securing an associated movement which, through conviction, would seek for the conformation of an agreement between State and Society; amongst public powers; amongst all government levels; amongst all social sectors. An agreement expressed through concrete actions within the family, the school, the neighborhood and the national and international society.

This public agreement should be supported by a policy that includes a mass media campaign to convey a profound message to the public at large; seeks that such media stop being the display window of the apology of both drug addiction and trafficking; and ensures that the principles and values that have enabled the continuation of the Species do not succumb by virtue of the poundings of the immorality of the ratings.

This public agreement should be founded also in an educational policy that would spread it to each educational center, in all levels and all grades, achieving a great collective consciousness. This public agreement should be beyond any ideological differences and of ordinary distances existing among parties, associations and political currents.

This public agreement is also amongst the legislative, the executive and the judicial branches of a State, wherein the autonomy of the government entities do not represent an excuse to miss a common purpose. This public agreement is a horizontal and vertical agreement; is an agreement that at the same time constitutes a bridge between State and Society, and between each State and all the others composing the hemispheric community and amongst all nations.

The promoters of the legalization, many of them in good faith, found their thesis in the assertion that for many years, programs to combat illicit drugs and drug trafficking have been developed nationally and internationally, and instead of alleviating these problems, they are globally more intense. Today, there are greater consumption, production, transferring, corruption, illness and violence.

In general terms, this assertion is not absent of veracity, however, it should not mean that the adequate solution is to simulate that the problem does not exist. What this assertion indicates is that a series of mistakes have been made and a series of deviations and excesses have resulted and impeded that the strategy of the combat of drugs becomes a reality.

The humanist policy that we propose is neither the strategy of prohibition, as such has been manifested so far; that is, on one side, it does not hides the existence of the problem and on the other, pursues to remedy the mistakes, deviations, excesses and deficiencies of the prohibitionists' theses that are applied in many countries.

In other words, the humanist policy regarding drug control does not mean to quit the fight against them; it does not imply that immature children and youth exercise their free will by choosing whether getting poisoned or not; whether wasting away and damage their social environment or not.

Here, the humanist policy of the State is to prevent this dilemma to appear, in general terms, without ignoring that since the beginning of the world, there have been persons that lose the way, faint in the quest; fail in the strengthening of their will and disregard the sense of sociability and solidarity.

Even reaching the extreme thesis, which by the way I do not share, that every individual is free to dispose without limitations of his/her body and of his/her own life, it cannot be overlooked that legally, no individual right, no personal liberty is absolute. Each of them implies a correspondent obligation: a particular concern cannot be above the public concern. Neither the most impetuous and extreme individual liberalism would be reasonably capable of invalidating the sociability formula which establishes that the limits of individual rights end at the commencement of the others' rights.

It is in this balance, in this interpretation of unities, where certain rights are interpreted in relation to others, where the hermeneutics of Human Rights really make sense. It is with this approach and under this vision that a humanist policy against illicit drugs should be spread. The humanist policy against illicit drugs, product of a Humanist State, is then a result of the public and social efforts to secure the force of Human Rights. Thus, this policy is not meant to debilitate the fight but instead, to redirect it to neutralize its adverse consequences and enhance its efficiency and effectiveness. In this way, our fight will be a fight for the dignity of the human person.

Then, let us say what a Humanist State with a humanist policy against drugs is, or maybe what it should be, although its enunciate is expressed in a catalogue-like presentation.

This policy:

1. Demands to treat the addict as an ill person, not as an offender; therefore, entails the guarantee of the right of health in an efficient manner, to those who requires of medical and psychological assistance.

2. Demands to identify the population that is potentially endangered by drug addiction and drug trafficking, particularly vulnerable groups like children, youth, elderly, indigenous people and those who suffer from any disability. Women of certain national societies would be included in this group. That is, the intention would be to give effect to the rights of gender, of the children and of neglected social groups.

3. Demands to make people aware of the harmful consequences of drugs, that is, ensuring the right to be informed.

4. Demands to avoid stigmatizing users, in order to secure the right to honor and reputation.

5. Demands that educational and informational policies as well as those related to drugs, do not give consideration to race, nationality, religion or any other that may represent an impairment to equality rights.

6. Demands to penalize, in a due process of law, with all formalities of legal proceedings, all those who produce, distribute and provide illicit drugs or chemical precursors for its manufacturing, launder funds, with penalties not unusual nor transcendent, and considering that incarceration penalties shall be aimed to the social rehabilitation of the offender; that is, the penalty shall only be imposed as a consequence of the existence of the Rule of Law and not as a consequence of a regime of exception.

7. Demands to consider reasons of equity whenever the offender has offended society by reason of poverty or ignorance.

8. Demands to make possible for those who plant and harvest illicit drugs, alternate cultivation that enable the men and women of the countryside to live with dignity and honor.

9. Demands to impede criminal organizations devoted to drug trafficking from associating with armed groups that endanger or clearly ignore the right to peace.

10. Demands to impede drug traffickers to threaten public safety which is a collective right that is inherent to us.

11. Demands that journalists be able to exercise their profession without being repressed or threatened, even when dealing with drug trafficking issues, so that the freedom of the press and the freedom of speech are not damaged.

On the other hand, the humanist policy facing the threat of drugs demands also the international cooperation, but this would represent a contradiction if used as a means of control and domination. The only valid international cooperation is the one based in respect to all countries, their territories, legal systems, forms of government, democratic institutions and life styles.

International cooperation within a humanist policy against illicit drugs should be capable of adding operating effectiveness to the political will; should be capable of identifying drug traffickers as the enemies and not the nations and governments that in spite of all their limitations, participate in the international effort; should be capable to avoid the simplicity of transferring own guilt to others in an effort to hide the internal costs and failures. The humanist policy against drugs does not certify, does not point out, does not stigmatize; on the contrary, makes evaluations in a participatory and inclusive manner, with the purpose of correcting; comprehends the levels of development of its partners, and is open to support from all.

Ladies and gentlemen, you may add much more to this proposal, as humble as incomplete. I leave it here for your reflection.

The huge interests that will have to be defeated to have and operate a humanist policy against drugs do not hide from me. These adverse interests will have to be publicly denounced, so that the fight against illicit drugs is not politically used to discuss any other type of controversies or simply to reach political power. The challenge is clear.

I am sure that in a world free of the drug threat, it will be much more easier to reach the guaranty of dignity of the human person, primary goal of the State and of the Humanist Society. Let us hope that it is in fact ahead. We in Mexico hope so.

IX: Future Challenges to Drug Control Policy

Rand Beers, Assistant Secretary, Department of State, United States

Biography

Rand Beers was sworn in as Assistant Secretary for International Narcotics and Law Enforcement Affairs on October 28, 1998. The Senate confirmed him on October 21, 1998. Mr. Beers is a member of the Senior Executive Service. He joined the Department of State in 1971 after four years in the U.S. Marine Corps. Before assuming his position as Assistant Secretary, Mr. Beers was the Principal Deputy Assistant Secretary for INL from January to October 1998. Mr. Beers served on the National Security Council (NSC) three times, recently as Special Assistant to the President and Senior Director for Intelligence Programs, and previously as Director for Global Issues and as Director for Counternarcotics and Counterterrorism. Mr. Beers also held various positions in the Bureau of Political Military Affairs of the Department of State: Deputy Assistant Secretary for Regional Affairs and Export Control, Deputy for Strategy and the Operations Coordinator for Regional Affairs and Security Assistance, Director of the Office of Security Analysis and the Office of International Security Policy, and Deputy Director of the Office of Policy Analysis. Additionally, he served as the Deputy Political Advisor to the Supreme Allied Commander, Europe. Mr. Beers was born in Washington, DC in 1942. He received a BA from Dartmouth in 1964 and an MA from the University of Michigan in 1971; both degrees in history. He is married and has two children.

CHANGING DYNAMICS OF THE INTERNATIONAL DRUG TRADE: CHALLENGES TO LEADERSHIP

I am very honored to have been invited to join two of the most distinguished leaders in the counternarcotics field to lead off the discussion of challenges for the future. I have tremendous respect and admiration for them, not only for what they have accomplished in their own countries, but for the tremendous contributions they have made to the anti-drug effort in the Western Hemisphere.

I will focus my comments on the narcotics control challenges that the international community is likely to encounter over the next three to five years and offer some (purposefully) provocative ideas on how we might organize ourselves to meet those challenges.

My basic assumptions are that:

♦ The international drug trade is poised to undergo a number of significant changes;

♦ Demand will grow, particularly in developing countries with large populations of young people and in areas experiencing political, economic, and social upheavals;

♦ The cocaine trade will continue to fragment into diverse production and trafficking patterns that are difficult to detect; non-Colombian groups will move into refinement and distribution.

♦ There will be a surge in other kinds of drugs to meet increasing world demand - heroin, but also an exponential increase in methamphetamine and other synthetic drugs.

Major cocaine traffickers, under continued governmental pressure, will:

♦ Move increasingly to remote and conflicted areas;

♦ Form alliances with other international organized crime factions, such as Asian and Russian groups; seek to secure distribution markets, leading to violence;

♦ Take even greater advantage of state-of-the-art technology to protect their shipments and launder their money; and

♦ Seek to diversify their operations into other kinds of drugs and other forms of crime, ranging from organized kidnapping and extortion to piracy of intellectual property.

Challenges:

We have to find ways to neutralize the advantages that traffickers have over governments in terms of flexibility in shifting routes and methods and their ability to make decisions rapidly, from operations to procurement decisions.

The continual emergence of new trafficking routes shows that there are few areas left in the world that are not directly tied into the illicit drug trade. The dispersal of routes is the traffickers' greatest advantage; it gives them tremendous flexibility and makes our work so much harder.

In addition, the traffickers' ability to keep pace with change has given them another advantage. Since money is no obstacle, they can acquire the latest equipment instantly. Governments, constrained by budgets, contracting regulations, and so forth, cannot adapt as quickly. And with new generations of technology arriving every 18 months or less, front-line authorities risk falling further and further behind.

Specifically, they are focusing their technology acquisitions on enhancing their operational security -- precision planning and timing, secure and rapid communications, improved knowledge of law enforcement's order of battle. In this regard, the widespread commercial availability of global positioning systems, cell phones, internet encryption, Internet faxing, and document reproduction equipment enables traffickers to envelop their operations quickly and cheaply in layers of security that are increasingly difficult for authorities to penetrate.

The technology contest between national authorities and traffickers is not new, but in the past, the advantage lay with the governments. What makes the problem so fundamentally different now, however, is the type of technology available to the traffickers - commercially or via other criminal groups -- and how fast it is advancing. Even fairly small trafficking groups can obtain sophisticated equipment and the major groups can generally out-spend the national authorities. Governments and traffickers are essentially competing for the same equipment.

Finding the Vulnerabilities:

A good drug strategy can exploit their vulnerabilities. A great drug strategy turns their own strengths against them. Visibility is the key. Our individual and collective efforts should focus on making the traffickers "visible."

Despite clandestine nature, safe havens and near-limitless resources of organized crime, not all of it is concealed in the criminal underground. Not all of it is mobile. Something is always visible.

The richer and more powerful they become, the more visible. They are businessmen with too many contacts. They must engage with the "open" economy to survive and that makes them vulnerable.

The more money they launder, the more visible they are.

Their luxury of ultimate flexibility and propensity to shift routes and methods In the face of even modest interdiction efforts, means that a concerted inter-governmental disruption campaign could keep them constantly off-guard and having to change their plans. They will begin to make mistakes. They will have to surface to regroup their operatives; they will be visible.

The more we know about legitimate commercial, banking, or transportation activity, the more visible the illicit activity will become. This applies to ports and airports as much as to banks, and may apply as well to the vendors of security technology.

And, key elements cannot survive without the protection of corrupt officials. With the right strategies and resources, and political courage, we can go back at these organizations through their minions within our own ranks.

<u>Strategic Focus:</u>

It is clearly very difficult to predict when, where, or how they will move. Still, we can watch for key indicators that give us warning and an idea of how to plan. In trying to forecast trends, there is no substitute for thorough analysis of seizure statistics, post-seizure intelligence, and informants. There is no substitute for investment in analytical capability. But, intelligence does not solve the drug problem. There are no easy solutions or infallible strategies.

First, we need to think about focusing on the most critical not necessarily the most vulnerable, aspects of the trade.

♦ How can we use their strengths against them as well as exploiting their weaknesses?

♦ How do we concentrate on those aspects of the trade that are essential for its long-term survivability?

♦ How do we expose the hidden or protected elements of these organizations? How do we strip away the protective layers of their public and private sector protectors?

Second, we should concentrate where we, the authorities, have -- or can gain -- a comparative information advantage. One important area is where the trade emerges from the underground into the mainstream of legitimate activity: areas such as banking, transportation, commercial shipping, and precursor chemicals. In this realm where records are kept and paper trails are created, low-profile regulators can have as much influence on crippling trafficking operations as more risk-prone law enforcement and other security forces.

Third, is the need to "know your trafficker". The only people who really know who the major traffickers are and how they operate are criminals themselves. It imperative that we have a way of penetrating these organizations, learning first hand about all aspects of their activities, and ultimately destroying them from inside and from the top down.

This requires effective laws, strong judicial systems, and good training. This involves skillful use of modern investigative techniques such as undercover operations, use of informants, controlled deliveries, wiretaps, and sting operations.

Use of plea-bargains or "rewards", combined with witness protection, can convince lower-level traffickers and lawyers or others involved with the cartels to assist law enforcement. It also requires the end to impunity. Major figures must be found and prosecuted. Those protecting the cartels must be exposed and punished. Extradition is a declaration by governments that their territory will not be a safe haven for criminals. All of these actions disrupt the organizations, and they serve as a deterrent to others who may be considering engaging in criminal activity.

Finally, the one area where we clearly have a technology advantage is through the use of communications networks to spread the anti-drug message. We call it Public Diplomacy. We cannot neglect efforts to reach opinion makers, the public, and our legislatures, both to gain support for our efforts and to promote greater awareness of many dangers that drug trafficking and abuse bring into our societies.

These are not unrealistic objectives. In fact, they are being increasingly used around the world with significant success. The greater the level of coordination between states, however, the greater the collective impact of our efforts.

Traffickers use our own borders and national sovereignty against us. The leadership challenge I want to put before you is how to achieve these objectives and to close the gaps between our borders and throughout our hemispheric waters and airspace and leave them no darkness in which to hide. How do we turn on the lights?

IX: Future Challenges to Drug Control Policy

Alejandro Aguinaga Recuenco, Minister of Health, Peru

Biography

Dr. Alejandro Aguinaga Recuenco currently serves as Peru's Minister of Health and as President of Contradrogas, Peru's antidrug coordinating agency. He previously served for 4 years as Vice Minister of Health. Prior to government service, Minister Aguinaga was a Resident in Surgical Medicine for five years at the Louis Pasteur University in Strasbourg, France. He also served on the Medical Faculty of Federico Villareal National University in Lima, Peru and as a Medical Intern at Ludwig Maximilian University in Munich, Germany. Dr. Aguinaga also earned an M.B.A. from the University of Saint Ingnacio Loyola in Peru.

FUTURE CHALLENGES OF DRUG CONTROL POLICY

Speech given by Dr. Alejandro Aguinaga,
Minister of Health and President of Drug Control,
at the Conference of Regional Drug Policy Leaders
(Washington, D.C., November 4 and 5, 1999)

Ladies and Gentlemen:

I would like to thank General McCaffrey for this invitation that provides an opportunity for a frank and open dialogue among drug control officials in the hemisphere.

We must prevent drug trafficking organizations, with their economic power, from winning the drug war and from continuing to gain ground because of shortcomings and limitations in our countries in organizing and coordinating efforts, and in using appropriate technologies and in financing.

Our major objective is for future generations to live in a better, drug-free world. Based on our experience and on the lessons learned, we must design and implement national and international strategies that are flexible, dynamic, and rigorous, to ensure effective action to put an end to the activities of criminal organizations that promote the production, trafficking, and use of drugs.

These strategies should be implemented on the basis of the following factors: a) development of a global design; b) a timely response capacity; c) sustainability of the results achieved; d) a firm attitude of rejection of drug use; and e) adequate financing. This is the challenge that we must respond to.

1. A global design for drug control

The drug threat and problem have moved well beyond the limits of the so-called consuming and producing countries to involve mankind as a whole. Countries which up to a short time ago were transit countries are now faced with alarming rates of increase in drug use. Other countries have become money laundering centers, and still others are now producers of synthetic drugs and/or suppliers of chemical precursors. Drug traffickers have globalized their operations, and so we, as the persons responsible for leading the fight against drugs, must implement a strategy of international cooperation and action that goes beyond borders.

Implementation of a global strategy and design must begin with the creation, ongoing revision, and/or strengthening of national and multinational agencies and cooperative organizations specializing in drug control. These entities should have the necessary political backing so that they can respond rapidly and effectively to the strategies of the drug traffickers.

2. A timely response capacity

Organized crime in the drug field responds very quickly to the strategies implemented by our countries to fight this scourge, by changing international routes and means of transport, promoting new areas for growing the illicit crops, using new types of chemical precursors, and developing new drugs. In Peru, for instance, effective prohibition of air space led to the use of rivers to transport drugs. The deterrent effect of the river prohibition program has led to a new approach, which is use of overland routes to the Peruvian coast, where the basic paste is processed into cocaine for shipment by sea. Traffickers have also varied their air traffic patterns and have replaced the Peru-Colombia route by an indirect routing through Brazil. This has had a direct impact on the price of coca leaves, which have exceeded profitability indices since mid-1998.

In order to have effective drug control, the law must have a highly flexible organization for the design, approval, and implementation of new strategies to offset the counter-strategies of the drug traffickers. In this regard, we should look into creating bilateral and multilateral coordination and decision-making mechanisms. These mechanisms should have the capacity to act fast in making and implementing decisions. They should be modeled along the lines of a task force, which can work without the encumbrance of bureaucratic restrictions, with full respect for national sovereignty and human rights. If we do not live in a state of constant alert and do not react immediately and forcefully, we will not win this battle.

Development of an adequate response capacity along these lines will help law enforcement officials have access to the means needed to improve their effectiveness. In other words, in order to globalize the fight against drugs and win it, it is essential to reduce the hemispheric imbalance in the supply of technology to support prohibition of drugs and chemical precursors, identify money laundering operations, prevent the illegal use of customs, monitor illicit crops, and increase the productivity of alternative crops, among other measures.

3. Ensuring the sustainability of results achieved in reducing the supply of crops for illicit use

In our efforts to reduce and eliminate illicitly used crops, it is crucial to have a balance between prohibition and alternative development.

If there are not adequate prohibitive measures that drastically reduce the profitability of illicit crops, the peasants will not be in a position to permanently abandon these crops, and if development of alternative crops is not sufficiently promoted, there is a risk that the peasants who have stopped growing the illicitly used crops will go back to them.

Our challenge is to obtain the necessary resources to maintain an adequate balance between the two policies, an essential foundation for an integral, sustainable strategy. In the case of coca producing countries, it is important to have a regional approach, so that production does not shift from one country to another.

However, a large part of the success or failure of the alternative development programs depends on the markets for alternative products in the countries of North America, Europe, and Asia. We appreciate the preferential tariff arrangements, and we hope that they will be extended until the alternative development programs are strengthened. We also believe that they need to be supplemented by creating a special mechanism to ensure that the products coming from the illicit crop zones have access to markets, and to encourage private investment and ensure that these products have the advantages they need to compete with the better prices and facilities offered to the peasants by drug traffickers.

4. Firm rejection of drug use

One critical challenge of undeniable importance is the need to create a strong determination to reject drug use. This should be done with the active participation of all civil society organized to fight this scourge.

Families, schools, universities, trade unions, the press, business associations, municipalities, and religious organizations should all play an active role in efforts to prevent drug use. Governments and leaders from different political parties should be aware of the social and economic costs involved in drug use, and of the fact that every dollar in their national budgets allocated to prevention represents a highly profitable social and economic investment which will benefit society as a whole.

I would ask that we join forces to initiate a movement to reject drugs, working closely with the media to encourage them to participate actively in a sustained, valiant effort.

5. Obtain adequate financing as part of a global effort

When the so-called consuming and producing countries decided to put an end to confrontation and mutual recrimination, and shifted to a position of "shared responsibility," a great step forward in the fight against drugs was taken and an atmosphere conducive to cooperation among all countries was created.

However, we need to embark on a new stage, one in which it is accepted that investment made by developed countries to supplement the limited resources of our countries is regarded as an investment to their own benefit and to the benefit of mankind as a whole, and not a gift. This should result in a substantial increase in the financing needed to sustain the fight against the production, trafficking, and use of drugs throughout the Americas. It should also reduce the huge imbalance between the northern and southern hemispheres in the availability of resources to fight drugs, which is not consistent with a global cost-benefit ratio at the present time.

Furthermore, arrangements to enable European countries to be more involved and participate more actively need to be improved, so that there is a better correlation between their participation and the demand for drugs which they generate. This effort should also include exports of inputs and chemical precursors.

Thank you very much.

X: Multilateral Evaluation Mechanism

Jean Fournier, Deputy Solicitor General, Canada

Biography

On November 4, 1993, Mr. Jean T. Fournier was appointed Deputy Solicitor General. Born in Quebec City in 1943, Mr. Fournier received his secondary education at Collêge Stanislas in Montreal. He has a B.A. from Queen's University and an M.A. in Economics from Laval University. He began his Federal Government career in 1968 as Special Assistant to the Minister of Indian Affairs and Northern Development. In 1978, Mr. Fournier was named Assistant Deputy Minister, Policy, Department of Communications, and served in this capacity until 1982 when he became Assistant Deputy Minister, Department of Finance. In 1986, Mr. Fournier was appointed Under-Secretary of State. In May 1998, Mr. Fournier was elected Chair of the Intergovernmental Working Group on the Multilateral Evaluation Mechanism (MEM) of the Inter-American Drug Abuse Control Commission (CICAD).

Introduction

Distinguished participants, ladies and gentlemen. As Chairman of the Intergovernmental Working Group on the Multilateral Evaluation Mechanism or MEM, I welcome this opportunity to talk to you today about an exciting and unprecedented achievement in hemispheric drug co-operation. It is appropriate that we discuss the MEM at the end of this conference. For the past two days discussions have ranged far and wide on the subject of future drug challenges in the hemisphere.

Building on the various presentations to date, I want to focus on an immediate and concrete subject-the MEM-which my colleagues and I who worked on it over the last sixteen months consider the anchor for renewed and strengthened efforts to address the drug issue into the next millennium.

The MEM embodies a change in the rhetoric of discussions on the drug problem, as does this conference. All 34 OAS countries are speaking a common language. We are linked by a common vision, that of a society increasingly free of the harmful effects of drugs. We are considering together the drug-related problems that affect all of our countries, all of our citizens, and we are doing it in a climate of co-operation. We are looking at the international drug problem and at transnational organized crime more generally, as a threat to the security of individuals, families and communities, as well as to our societies and our governments.

On September 2 in Ottawa, delegates from all member-countries reached agreement on the MEM-- some referred to it as the 'Spirit of Ottawa' -- which promises to be a powerful new tool in the fight against the threat to human security posed by the traffic in, and abuse of, illicit drugs. It will help develop stronger and better partnerships between countries, and between their health and law enforcement officials.

In Montevideo just weeks ago, the CICAD Commission formally adopted the MEM and the implementation phase has already begun. Let me take a few minutes to describe for you what the MEM is, why it marks a milestone in hemispheric co-operation on the drug issue and what all of us need to do to ensure that the extraordinary levels of co-operation exhibited to date in the development of the MEM, continues through the first round of evaluation, leading to the next Summit of the Americas, in Quebec City, in 2001.

The Historical Context

The Spirit of Ottawa and its momentum can be clearly traced to some key events over the last five years. Leaders, presidents and prime ministers representing all 34 OAS member countries have twice come together at a Summit of the Americas. The drug problem was on the agenda of both Summits. The first Summit was in Miami in 1994, followed by a second Summit in Santiago, Chile in April 1998.

At the Miami Summit, leaders agreed to put an end to the era of finger-pointing at countries that were either producers, consumers or transit points of illicit drugs. They accepted the principle of shared responsibility and recognized that international co-operation is essential to stop the transnational movement of illegal drugs. And that's when they asked CICAD to develop a hemisphere-wide drug strategy.

Two years later in 1996, member-countries adopted a comprehensive and balanced Anti-Drug Strategy for the Hemisphere. That strategy represented a major commitment to address the diverse nature of the drug problem, and it set out shared goals to reduce both the supply of, and demand for, drugs and to improve control measures.

At the Santiago Summit last year, leaders recognized that measures to fight the flow of illicit drugs between countries in the Americas needed to be taken one step further. They again turned to CICAD and asked it to establish a mechanism to evaluate and strengthen individual and collective efforts against drugs.

Shortly after the Summit, the Intergovernmental Group was formed and I was honored to be elected as its Chair and my colleague, Pablo Lagos of Chile, as Vice-Chair.

Our task was to create a MEM designed by all, for all, so that every country's efforts could be measured objectively based on the four elements of the OAS's Anti-Drug Strategy; namely, strengthening anti-drug plans; prevention and treatment; reduction in drug production; and, improved law enforcement. As our work progressed, we realized that we needed to deal with another issue as well: measuring the social and economic costs of the drug problem, an issue we discussed here yesterday.

Working Group Objectives for the MEM

The Working Group's starting point in developing the MEM sixteen months ago was a common vision, that of a society increasingly free of drugs; as well as a common strategy to implement that vision, the 1996 Anti-Drug Strategy in the Hemisphere.

From there we proceeded to obtain agreement on a set of principles. These would be the foundation of our work. They included concepts such as shared responsibility, respect for sovereignty and an integrated, balanced approach that focuses at the same time on the production, trafficking and consumption of illicit drugs.

Second, we agreed to a number of characteristics of the MEM. We spoke of a MEM that is governmental, singular and objective, and that involves the full participation of the member states. We agreed that this mechanism was about sharing responsibility, not imposing sanctions or attributing blame. The MEM is seen as a forum for all countries to openly discuss how best to work together in a professional and respectful manner, to share best practices and to learn from each other.

Third, we agreed to objectives that define what we want the MEM to achieve. These highlight the benefits of the MEM for individual states and for the entire hemisphere. For example, a key objective of the MEM is to strengthen mutual dialogue and co-operation in the hemisphere in dealing with the diverse aspects of the drug problem.

We recognize that borders and sovereignty are important for nation states but that it is equally important that borders not represent bridges for criminals and walls for law enforcement authorities wrestling with drug trafficking, organized crime or terrorism. New and enhanced forms of cross-border collaboration across the hemisphere on the drug problem are not just desirable, they are essential! Collaboration improves outcomes, as we all know.

Evaluating progress: Indicators

From these building blocks, the MEM began to take shape and the Working Group then turned its attention to the translation of the Anti-Drug Strategy into a coherent set of critical indicators within each of the four elements of the Strategy. The indicators are a powerful new tool that will allow countries to evaluate individual and collective progress of anti-drug efforts to a common standard. Most important, the indicators will help us determine whether the actions we are taking are effective in achieving the objectives of the Hemispheric Strategy. Indicators are like pieces of a puzzle. When put together, they provide a picture of the whole of the progress we are making and the challenges that lie ahead.

After lengthy and detailed discussions, the Working Group agreed on 79 indicators that will form the basis of the evaluation and of the questionnaire that will be completed by member-countries. The indicators will provide a practical and objective means of evaluating progress against illicit drugs, while at the same time identifying areas where countries require greater effort.

As well, the indicators will help us maintain a balanced approach to the drug issue. And they will show us how our efforts compare to what each other is doing and how we can help each other strengthen our National Anti-Drug Plans. Information sharing and benchmarking will help all countries to improve their performance. What gets evaluated gets attention.

While indicators have been used in other areas of international co-operation, such as the OECD and the IMF, this is the first time that indicators are being applied to the area of illicit drugs.

For instance, one indicator requires countries to report the number of drug seizure operations by law enforcement agencies, and the quantities of drugs seized. That indicator will provide information on the progress in stemming drug trafficking.

To assess progress on reducing drug demand, there is an indicator that asks countries whether they have drug treatment and rehabilitation programs that include early intervention, outreach and social re-integration of drug users. The police have consistently pointed to these programs as an essential part of the community response to the drug issue.

In today's world, having indicators and performance measures is the cornerstone of an enterprise's current and future success. Whether one is a senior executive in government or industry, timely and reliable performance measures are needed to make informed judgements about increasingly complex issues. Therefore, the ability to gather, arrange and manipulate vast quantities of information is essential to sound management decisions. This is why the MEM is so important, as are the 79 indicators we have selected.

These indicators will provide CICAD with a much-needed foundation and performance information on country and hemispheric anti-drug efforts, and have the capacity to become over time an essential part of the Western Hemisphere's drug diagnostic tool kit.

Without well-thought out indicators there can be no sensible change or improvement in the way we do things. Indicators are like a compass to the captain. They guide us, and tell us if we are heading in the right direction. Without them, progress is impossible to gauge. Quite simply, if you don't know where you are going, you will never get there.

Put differently, indicators may be likened to the measurements a doctor takes on a routine physical examination: weight, pulse, temperature, and blood pressure. The readings show him what we need to find out and what remedial action we need to take.

Finally, the indicators should prove invaluable in dealing with some of the challenges we have discussed here over the last two days: future trends in drug use, the impact of drugs on public health, what strategies law enforcement agencies should be considering and adopting, and the social and economic costs of drugs.

First Round of Evaluation

Having selected a comprehensive set of indicators, the Working Group approved the format of the questionnaire for the gathering of information and agreed to an evaluation procedure and timetable.

The first round of evaluation will take place in year 2000, using a reduced list of 61 indicators to establish an information base that will serve to measure future progress. Other indicators will be added later as we gain experience. This is simply a case of us learning to walk before running.

The Working Group also agreed that the first round of evaluation would be carried out by a Government Expert Group (GEG) formed by 34 experts, one from each country. The GEG will determine its own organization and procedures, and will have the responsibility of preparing the evaluation report for each country and a hemispheric report which will be presented to the CICAD Commission for its approval at the end of year 2000.

Final evaluation reports, which will include findings and recommendations, will be made public. It is intended that the first round of testing of the new mechanism will be completed in time for the next Summit of the Americas in Quebec City (Canada) in 2001, when the drug issue and the MEM are expected to be key issues for discussion among the 34 leaders of the hemisphere.

Recognizing that the MEM is a living mechanism and that changes will likely be required to the MEM to reflect the lessons of the first round, CICAD therefore agreed that the Working Group would be called back as required over the next year to consider these changes.

Finally, it was agreed that a MEM support unit would be created within the CICAD Executive Secretariat to assist the experts in their work. David Beall will have more to say in a moment about the work of the MEM support group and the details of implementing the MEM.

Conclusion

In conclusion, allow me to share a few thoughts with you on next steps and the conditions as I see them for the successful implementation of the MEM.

The importance of working together across the world on the drug issue has never been clearer. Several weeks ago, I traveled to Europe to meet with a number of key partners in the global fight against drugs. I met with officials of the European Commission, the United Nations, Europol and the European Monitoring Centre on Drugs and Drug Addiction. They showed considerable interest and support for CICAD's achievements and expressed the hope that the MEM would become global.

Our colleagues marveled at how 34 diverse countries in the hemisphere were able to come together so quickly on such a politically sensitive and highly emotional issue. They wondered about how we were able to achieve so much in a short period of time, and in a truly remarkable spirit of co-operation and 'esprit de corps.' I pointed out that the Working Group's achievement was made possible by the extraordinary degree of political commitment in all the capitals, at the highest levels, to make the MEM succeed.

This leads me to three important points that are crucial to fulfilling our objective of implementing an effective MEM.

First, the adoption of the MEM at Montevideo was not the end but only the end of the beginning. There is a great deal of work to do to realize the MEM to its full potential and to have for the next Summit of the Americas, country reports and a hemispheric report that are intelligible in their analysis and practical, credible and even-handed in their recommendations.

The MEM architecture is complete, now it is time for the "people" to move in. It is imperative that each country assign an expert to the Governmental Experts Group and do so without delay to begin work on the evaluation. To deliver an effective and credible product to leaders in Quebec City in 2001, the MEM train has to leave the station soon and with all the people, and the right people, on board.

Second, there is the issue of funding for this work. During the MEM deliberations, the Working Group agreed that countries would pay for their representative to participate in the experts group and that a solidarity fund would be established to ensure the involvement of those countries, that, owing to exceptional circumstances, might otherwise be unable to participate. Significant funding pledges have been obtained to cover the costs of implementing the MEM. Additional funds are needed.

I think it is important that, to truly represent the spirit of 'by all for all', every country contribute, commensurate with their ability, to the funding of this work.

Third, it is equally important that countries continue to provide leadership at the highest levels -- from Ministers and their deputies -- to ensure consistent support for the MEM implementation process. I would urge each of you to consider the successful implementation of the MEM as a personal goal.

We are here today linked by a common vision and determination to make the right things happen. MEM is one of those things. We need your continuing support and leadership to ensure that each of our needs and expectations can be fully realized-and by looking around this room I know those here today can make that goal a reality.

In closing, I wish to acknowledge the concerted efforts of all member states and the work of their delegations in bringing the MEM to fruition. As well, I want to acknowledge the unwavering support of the Secretary General of the OAS throughout this endeavor. On behalf of the Working Group, Pablo Lagos and I also want to extend special thanks and appreciation to Mr. David Beall, Mr. Alberto Hart and their staff, for their excellent support over the last sixteen months.

XI: Conference Summation and Closing Remarks

Barry R. McCaffrey, Director Office of National Drug Control Policy

CONCLUDING POINTS
WESTERN HEMISPHERE DRUG POLICY LEADERSHIP CONFERENCE
NOVEMBER 5, 1999

OVERVIEW—

- This first-ever Western Hemisphere Drug Policy Leadership Conference takes place almost precisely between the Santiago 2nd Summit of the Americas in April 1998 and the Quebec City 3rd Summit of the Americas scheduled for April 2001.

- Our conference has brought together the men and women who, following the Santiago Summit Mandate, negotiated the Multilateral Evaluation Mechanism, a hemispheric performance measurement system. The MEM will be implemented during year 2000.

- The MEM will help to create a new hemispheric counterdrug relationship focused on the common problem of drugs and based on mutual respect and cooperation.

- As we prepare for this new stage, we thought it important to take stock of how far we have come and to lay out the new challenges we will face in the next decade.

- Over the past three days we have heard presentations from the hemisphere's top counter-drug experts—both demand and supply.

- These presentations have generated thorough discussion and led to emergence of consensus on a number of important principles. Below these key issues are highlighted by topic.

FUTURE CHANGES IN DRUG USE: PATTERNS AND TRENDS

Key Points—

1. **Drug consumption growing:** It is becoming major problem throughout hemisphere. For the first time many South American countries are measuring significant increase in use of illicit drugs, including cocaine and heroin.

2. **Education is critical:** Need to make clear the social and economic consequences of drug abuse to society and develop targeted programs to different segments of the population.

3. **Need high quality treatment:** Nations must implement universal standards to improve quality and consistency of drug treatment service delivery.

4. **Coordination is essential:** Need for better interagency integration of demand reduction programs; and to balance those programs with supply reduction for an integrated national policy.

RESEARCH AND SCIENCE: PUBLIC HEALTH IMPACT OF DRUG ABUSE

Key Points—

1. **Addiction is a brain disease:** People who take drugs are self-medicating to make themselves feel good (increase dopamine levels). They take drugs to chemically induce pleasure. The result is that regular drug users modify the state of their brains. A major task of treatment is to get brain back to normal. Compulsive drug use brings misery to addicts.

2. **Drug addiction is a treatable disease:** Scientific research provides effective, proven tools to treat those addicted to drugs.

3. **We know how to lower risk of drug abuse:** Protective or resiliency factors that reduce risk of addiction include strong families, and education, as well as multiple affiliations with organized entities such as schools, churches and athletics.

4. **Drug abuse and crime are linked:** Research indicates that 70% of incarcerated inmates testing positive for drugs will return to prison if treatment is not provided to them.

5. **We must disseminate what we learn:** Research results on prevention, education and treatment should be disseminated, in appropriate languages, throughout hemisphere.

CURRENT AND FUTURE TRENDS IN DRUG TRAFFICKING

Key Points—

1. **Drug trafficking is a big business:** Narcotraffickers want to make money. Law enforcement should give high priority to following the money—asset forfeiture is the way to get at the leadership of major drug trafficking organizations.

2. **Private sector can help:** Law enforcement must open doors to business and civil society—build bridges to gather information and support. Cooperation of financial institutions is an essential component to effective drug enforcement.

3. **What we measure is critical:** Seizure statistics and analysis should be used differently, not as body count. Seizures, properly analyzed and exploited, can lead to important information, arrests and act as a deterrent.

4. **Personnel issues central to mission:** Must devote necessary resources to hire, train, and equip police, judicial, and customs officials. The quality of police forces, their investigative capabilities and their immunity to corruption are crucial to counterdrug law enforcement. Regional centers for training, education, and information sharing can help.

LAW ENFORCEMENT STRATEGIES FOR THE FUTURE

Key Points—

1. **Standardize legal framework:** Every nation needs the ability to conduct complex investigations of criminal organizations. Useful tools in these investigations include undercover operations and extradition.

2. **Globalization of drug trade requires cooperation:** Law enforcement must change – to include: interdependence, increased collaboration, and more rapid exchange of information and intelligence. Operatives must be trained in high technology. Illicit drugs are the major source of income to international criminal groups. International cooperation is key to effectively targeting them.

3. **Anti-corruption measures:** Transnational crime and narcotrafficking are creating parallel state structures that compromise the legitimate government. In addition, drug money is now used to commercialize legitimate activity. The result is that the rule of law and democracy are undermined.

4. **Law Enforcement must work with the protected civilian community:** Agencies must engage and participate with wider society through public education and mobilization as well as through community policing.

SOCIAL AND ECONOMIC COSTS OF DRUGS

Key Points—

1. **Policy should be driven by data:** Strengthening scientific institutions and developing solid data can increase society understanding of drug-related problems.

2. **Technical Assistance needed to measure costs:** Tools to measure social costs of drugs are only now being developed and used. Many countries need assistance/training to enable them to develop their own expertise.

3. **Rivalry between resources for supply and demand reduction is unhelpful:** There are social costs for societies due to both drug trafficking and drug consumption. Need to measure costs and seek solution to both sets of challenges.

THE NATIONAL YOUTH ANTI-DRUG MEDIA CAMPAIGN

Key points—

1. **Approach to campaign design involves:** Forming alliances; involving the local private sector; partnering with media owners; working with the advertising industry; and using market research.

2. **U.S. experience shows value of:** Integrated marketing and public health communications campaign; targeting multiple audiences reached where they live, work and play (via internet, movies, classrooms, televisions, etc.); and, employing culturally relevant messages in appropriate languages.

3. **Must study impact and continually update campaign via:** Awareness and attitude tracking 365 days per year and using communications mapping (to illustrate which media vehicle is most effective in communicating each message).

FUTURE CHALLENGES TO DRUG CONTROL POLICY

Key Points—

1. **Need to set goals:** The Multilateral Evaluation Mechanism will be an important international assessment method. There is also need for individual countries to set achievable goals in their national strategies and measure efforts to meet them.

2. **Traffickers are developing new products:** Today's traffickers are savvy marketers and business experts. They are diversifying product line, exploiting new markets, introducing synthetic drugs and involving themselves in a broader array of criminal activities.

3. **Corruption can undermine our efforts:** Nations need to reward and protect individuals who reveal corruption and to conduct public audits on the expenditure of drug-related government funds.

4. **Justice system as a whole must work:** We cannot just arrest people. We must have strong prosecutors and judges as well as effective prison system.

5. **Hemisphere must transcend national borders:** Nations cannot let drug traffickers exploit national borders. We must work together regionally and hemispherically to go after traffickers.

6. **Role of free press must be protected:** Journalists covering counterdrug efforts play a critical role in educating public. Their physical safety and the right to do their jobs must be protected.

MULTILATERAL EVALUATION MECHANISM

Key Points—

1. **MEM is an historic achievement:** No large group of nations has ever attempted such a multifaceted mutual evaluation system. All 34 OAS countries are united in a common recognition of the problem. We are linked by a common vision. The rest of the world is watching with interest.

2. **We will learn a lot in first year:** In calendar 2000 MEM will use 61 of 82 indicators. We must walk before we can run. We will present year 2000 results to the hemispheric heads of government in Quebec City at the 3rd Summit of the Americas. With their approval, we will apply what we have learned and do better in 2001.

3. **MEM will focus national governments:** Many nations need to develop the technical capacity to measure consumption, to provide quality treatment, to control drug and chemical trafficking and address money laundering. We will learn from and help each other.

4. **Hemispheric nations can only make informed decision with good data:** In both government or industry — timely and reliable performance measures are needed to make informed judgements. The ability to gather, arrange and manipulate vast quantities of information is essential to sound anti-drug management decisions. That is why the MEM is so important.

RECOMMENDATIONS:

During discussion, senior drug policy leaders reached consensus that we would:

⇒ Meet again, subject to CICAD's call, to assess our progress and challenges.

⇒ Discourage the legalization of drugs due to the severe health threat posed by consumption of illicit narcotics.

⇒ Share information about successful antidrug programs.

⇒ Coordinate and cooperate regionally and hemispherically on interdiction of drugs, chemicals, and money.

⇒ Develop tailored anti-drug media campaigns that effectively make use of television, radio, internet, magazines.

⇒ Increase prevention and education information available on the Internet.

⇒ Encourage treatment of those in prison or under criminal justice supervision.

⇒ Above all, to aggressively support the multilateral spirit and momentum that we have achieved.

CONCLUSION:

• Thank you, finally, to David Beall, Alberto Hart and the entire CICAD Executive Secretariat for their hard work is putting this event together.

• Let me conclude with the insightful words of U.S. Assistant Secretary of State for Global Affairs, Thomas Pickering, who told us during the Heads of Delegation Conference Dinner:

> *"Narcotics trafficking is simply too large, too complex, and too fluid a problem to be tackled by any one country or small group of countries. Only as true partners working together on all fronts can we hope to meet and effectively beat back the daunting global drug challenge. This is a true partnership and reflects an unprecedented level of mutual trust and confidence in the future. It will serve as a model for other regions and for the global community."*

Appendices

Western Hemisphere Drug Policy Leadership Conference

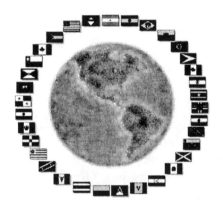

Washington, D.C.

November 3-5, 1999

Conference Agenda

Wednesday, November 3, 1999

16:30 – 18:00 Registration of Participants
18:00 – 20:00 Reception - Blue Room
21:00   Heads of Delegation Dinner - New Heights Restaurant
               Thomas Pickering, Under Secretary of State for Political Affairs,
               United States

Thursday, November 4, 1999

08:00 – 09:00 Registration of Participants

09:00 – 09:30 Inaugural Session/Welcome - Palladian Room
               Barry R. McCaffrey, Director, Office for National Drug Control Policy (ONDCP),
               United States
               David R. Beall, Executive Secretary, Inter-American Drug Abuse Control
               Commission (CICAD), OAS

09:30 – 10:00 Presentation I: Future Changes in Drug Use: Patterns and Trends
               Augusto Perez Gomez, Dircctor, President's Program to Confront Drug
               Consumption, Colombia
               Jorge Bolivar Diaz, Assistant Executive Secretary, SECCATID, Guatemala

10:00 – 10:45 Discussion by participants
10:45 – 11:00 Recess
11:00 – 11:30 Presentation II: Research and Science: Public Health Impact of Drug Abuse and
               Addiction
               Alan Leshner, Director, National Inst. on Drug Abuse (NIDA), US

11:30 – 12:15 Discussion by participants
12:15 – 13:45 Lunch - Blue Room
               Introduction of Presentation on Anti-Drug Media Campaign by Dr. Leshner
               Shona Seifert, Senior Partner, Ogilvy & Mather

13:45 – 14:15 Presentation III: Current and Future Trends in Drug Trafficking
               Ronald K. Noble, Secretary General ICPO-Interpol – nominee
14:15 – 15:00 Discussion by participants
15:00 – 15:15 Recess
15:15 – 15:45 Presentation IV: Law Enforcement Strategies for the Future
               Walter Maierovitch, Secretary, National Antidrug Secretariat, (SENAD), Brazil
               Joseph Theodore, Minister of National Security, Trinidad & Tobago

15:45 – 16:30   Discussion by participants

16:30 – 17:00   Presentation V: Social and Economic Costs of Drugs
                Eduardo Amadeo, Secretary, National Anti-Drug Secretariat, (SEDRONAR),
                Argentina
                Jacques LeCavalier, Chief Executive Officer Canadian Centre on Substance Abuse
                (CCSA), Canada
                Claudio Molina, Counselor, National Drug Control Agency, (CONACE), Chile
17:00 – 17:30   Discussion by participants

17:30 – 18:00   Synthesis and Summation of Discussions
                Alberto Scavarelli, Vice Minister, National Drug Prevention and Control Agency,
                Office of the President, Uruguay

18:00   Adjournment

19:00 – 21:00   Conference Dinner - Diplomat Room
                Introduction by General McCaffrey via video tape
                Jorge Quiroga, Vice President, Republic of Bolivia

Friday, November 5, 1999

08:30–09:00   Presentation VI: Future Challenges to Drug Control Policy
                Jorge Madrazo Cuellar, Attorney General, México
                Rand Beers, Assistant Secretary, Department of State, U.S.
                Dr. Alejandro Aguinaga, Ministro de Salud y Presidente de Contradrogas, con
                motivo de la Conferencia de Líderes del Hemisferio sobre Politicas de Drogas,
                Peru

09:00 – 09:30   Discussion by participants

09:30 –10:00   Presentation VII: Multilateral Evaluation Mechanism
                Jean Fournier, Deputy Solicitor General, Canada
                David Beall, Executive Secretary, CICAD/OAS

10:00 – 10:30   Discussion by participants
10:30 – 10:45   Recess

10:45 – 11:30   Conference Summation and Closing Remarks
                Barry R. McCaffrey, Director, ONDCP

11:30 – 12:00   Conference Photograph
12:00 – 13:00   Closing Press Conference - Palladian Room
                Barry R. McCaffrey, Director ONDCP
                Dr. César Gaviria, Secretary General, OAS

Western Hemisphere Drug Policy Leadership Conference

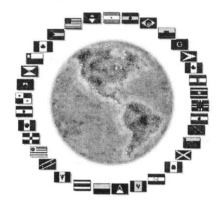

Washington, D.C.

November 3-5, 1999

Country Delegations

ANTIGUA AND BARBUDA

Bernard S. Percival
Minister of Health and Social Improvement
Tel: (268) 460 - 9425
Fax: (268) 462 - 5003
E-mail: antiguaedu@candw.ag

Lionel A. Hurst
Ambassador, Permanent Representative of Antigua and Barbuda to the OAS
Tel: (202) 362 - 5122
Fax: (202) 362 - 5225
E-mail: MaxHurst@aol.com

ARGENTINA

Eduardo Amadeo
Secretario de Estado - Secretaría de Programación para la Prevención de la
Drogadicción y la Lucha Contra el Narcotrafico (SEDRONAR)
Tel: (54-114) 320 - 1250
Fax: (54-114) 325 - 9499
E-mail: cedetuid@sedronar.gov.ar

Juan Minieri Saint-Beat
Consejero de la Embajada Argentina ante los Estados Unidos
E-mail: JMMWASH@AOL.COM

Martín Gómez Bustillo
Consejero, Representante Alterno de Argentina ante la OEA
Tel: (202) 387 - 4142
Fax: (202) 387 - 4142
E-mail: JMMWASH@AOL.COM

COMMONWEALTH of the BAHAMAS

Frank Watson
Deputy Prime Minister and Minister of National Security
Tel: (242) 356 - 6801

Peter Deveaux-Isaacs
Deputy Permanent Secretary, Ministry of Foreign Affairs
Tel: (242) 322 - 7624
Fax: (242) 328 - 8212
E-mail: esq.pdi@batelnet

Sir Arlington Butler
Ambassador - Permanent Representative of Bahamas to the OAS
Tel: (202) 319 - 2660 ext. 618
Fax: (202) 319 - 2668

Marvin Hanlon Dames
Deputy Superintendent of Police - Royal Bahamas Police Force
Tel: (242) 322 - 2919

William Weeks
Executive Director - National Drug Council (NIDC)
Tel: (809) 325 - 4633/4
Fax: (809) 325 - 8442

BARBADOS

Joseph Atherley, MP
Parliamentary Secretary - Office of the Attorney General and Ministry of Home Affairs
Tel: (246) 228 - 0284
Fax: (246) 228 - 5433
E-mail: mha@caribsurf.com

Joyce Bourne
First Secretary, Alternate Representative of Barbados to the OAS
Tel: (202) 939 - 9200
Fax: (202) 332 - 7467
E-mail: barbados@oas.org

BELIZE

Jules Vasquez
Chairman - National Drug Abuse Control Council (NDACC)
    Tel: (501-2) 31-125/ 31-143/ 31-106
    Fax: (501-2) 31-121
    E-mail: ndacc@btl.net

Ornel Brooks
Director - National Drug Abuse Control Council (NDACC)
    Tel: (501-2) 31-125/ 31-143/ 31-106
    Fax: (501-2) 31-121
    E-mail: ndacc@btl.net

BOLIVIA

Jorge Quiroga
Vicepresidente de la República de Bolivia
    Tel: (202) 785 - 0219

Walter Guiteras
Ministro de Gobierno
    Tel: (591-2) 41-0300/ 41-1126/ 41-0870
    Fax: (591-2) 41-9973
    E-mail: socidef@ceibo.entelnet.bo

Guillermo Canedo
Viceministro de Defensa Social
    Tel: (591) 241 - 0330 / 241 - 1126 / 241 - 0870
    Fax: (591) 241 - 9973
    E-mail: icinal@entelnet.bo

Sergio Medinacelli
Viceministro de Prevención y Rehabilitación
    Tel: (591) 239 - 0988
    E-mail: vmprs@kolla.net

Marlene Fernández del Granado
Embajadora, Representante Permanente de Bolivia ante la OEA
    Tel: (202) 785 - 0219
    Fax: (202) 296 - 0563

Mary Carrasco
Directora General de Asuntos Especiales y Relaciones con Estados Unidos
    Tel: (591-2) 370 - 195
    Fax: (591-2) 365 – 590

Alberto Quiroga
Ministro Consejero– Representante Alterno de Bolivia ante la OEA
    Tel: (202) 785- 0219
    Fax: (202) 296 - 0563

Erich R. Kuhn
Ministro Consejero – Embajada de Bolivia ante los Estados Unidos
    Tel: (202) 483 - 4410
    Fax: (202) 328 - 3712

Francisco Roque
Consejero Antinarcoticos y Político – Embajada de Bolivia ante los Estados Unidos
    Tel: (202) 483 - 4410
    Fax: (202) 328 - 3712

Carmen Henry
Segundo Secretario - Embajada de Bolivia ante los Estados Unidos
    Tel: (202) 483 - 4410
    Fax: (202) 413 - 4665

Yuri Monje
Segundo Secretario, Representante Alterno de Bolivia ante la OEA
    Tel: (202) 785 - 0218 / 785 - 0219
    Fax: (202) 296 - 0563
    E-mail: monje001@hotmail.com

BRAZIL

Wálter Fanganiello Maierovitch
Director - Secretário Nacional Antidrogas (SENAD)
    Tel: (55-61) 411 - 2152/ 411 - 2097
    Fax: (55-61) 411 - 2053/ 411 - 2110
    E-mail: senad@planalto.gov.br
             mariaertb@planalto.gov.br

Michael Gepp
Asistente - Internationão da Secretaria Nacional Antidrogas
    Tel: (55-61) 411 - 2074/ 411 - 2 097
    Fax: (55-61) 411 - 2053/ 411 - 2110
    E-mail: michaelfmm@plavello.gob.br

Carlo Alberto Leite Barbosa
Embaixador - Embaixada do Brasil em Washington
    Tel: (202) 238 - 2700
    Fax: (202) 238 - 2827

Julio Bitelli
Embaixada do Brasil em Washington
    Tel: (202) 238 - 2700
    Fax: (202) 238 - 2827
    E-mail: bitelli@brasilemb.org

Aldemo Garcia Junior
Primeiro Secretário - Representante Suplente do Brasil Junto à CICAD
    Tel: (202) 333 - 4224 / 333 - 4225
    Fax: (202) 333 - 6610

Monica Fonseca Gill
Coordinador de Comunicao local
Tel.   (55-61) 411 - 2057

CANADA

Jean T. Fournier
Deputy Solicitor General - Office of the Solicitor General Canada, and
Principal Representative of Canada to CICAD and
Chairman of the Intergovernmental Working Group on the
Multilateral Evaluation Mechanism (MEM)
Tel: (613) 991 - 2895
Fax: (613) 990 - 8312
E-mail: FournieJ@sgc.gc.ca

Diane Jacovella
Associate Director - Ministry of Health
Tel: (613) 957 - 8337
E-mail: diane-jacovelle@hc-sc.gc.ca

Philip Pinnington
Directeur adjoint Direction du crime international (AGC) - Department of Foreign Affairs and International
Trade (DFAIT)
Tel: (613) 996 - 0444
Fax: (613) 996 - 0444
E-mail: Philip.Pinnington@dfait-maeci.gc.ca

Jo-Anne Tremblay
Senior Executive Assistant - Office of the Deputy Solicitor General
Tel: (613) 991 - 2895
Fax: (613) 990 - 8312
E-mail: tremblj@sgc.gc.ca

Michel Perron
Chief Executive Officer - Canadian Centre on Substance Abuse
Tel: (613) 235 - 4048 ext. 227
Fax: (613) 235 - 8101
E-mail: mperron@ccsa.ca

Jacques LeCavalier
Former Chief Executive Officer – Canadian Centre on Substance Abuse
Tel: (613) 235 - 4048 ext. 229
Fax: (613) 235 - 8101
E-mail: jlecaval@ccsa.ca

CHILE

Pablo Lagos
Secretario Ejecutivo - Consejo Nacional para el Control de Estupefacientes (CONACE)
    Tel: (562) 510 - 0800 / 510 - 0810
    Fax: (562) 671- 6922
    E-mail: plagos@conace.cl

Guillermo Anguita
Consejero - Embajada de Chile ante los Estados Unidos
    Tel: (202) 785 - 1746
    Fax: (202) 887 - 5579
    E-mail: gar_echileus@radix.net

Frederick Heller
Primer Secretario - Representante Alterno de Chile ante la OEA
    Tel: (202) 887 - 5475 / 887 - 5476
    Fax: (202) 775 - 0713
    E-mail: vvilugro@segegob.cl

Claudio Molina Diaz
Asesor Consejero - (CONACE)
    Tel: (562) 510 - 0800
    Fax: (562) 671 - 6922
    E-mail: cmolina@conace.gov.cl

COLOMBIA

Mauricio González Cuervo
Viceministro de Justicia y del Derecho
    Tel: (571) 334 - 4037 / 342 - 8714 / 342 - 8659
    Fax: (571) 281 - 55 79

Gabriel Merchán Benavides
Director - Consejo Nacional de Estupefacientes
    Tel: (571) 636 - 2139 / 691 - 6603
    Fax: (571) 257 - 8416
    E-mail: 104551.3479@compuserve.com

Ismael Trujillo Polanco
Brigadier General – Policía Nacional de Colombia
    Tel: (571) 280 - 4950 / 280 - 0358

Augusto Pérez Gómez
Director – Programa Presidencial para Enfrentar el Consumo de Drogas
Adriana Mendoza
Consejera de la Embajada de Colombia ante los Estados Unidos
    Tel: (202) 387 - 8338
    E-mail: am@colombiaemb.org

Isaura Duarte Rodríguez
Segunda Secretaria – Representante Alterna de Colombia ante la OEA
    Tel: (202) 332 - 8003 / 332 - 8004
    Fax: (202) 234 - 9781
    E-mail: col-oas2@erols.com

COSTA RICA

Rogelio Ramos
Viceministro de la Presidencia - Presidente de Centro Nacional de Prevención contra Drogas (CENADRO)
    Tel: (506) 280 - 9618
    Fax: (506) 280 - 9618
    E-mail: rramos@gobnet.go.cr

Carlos Arias Nuñez
Fiscal General de la República
    Tel: (506) 295 - 3458

Eugenia Mata Chavarría
Jefe de Proyectos del Centro Nacional de Prevención Contra Drogas (CENADRO)
    Tel: (506) 258 - 4072 / 73
    E-mail: cenadro@sol.racsa.co

Edwin Araya Quiros
Asesor al Presidente del Centro Nacional de Prevención contra Drogas (CENADRO)
    Tel: (506) 280 - 9618
    Fax: (506) 280 - 9618

Erika Harms
Ministro Consejero y Subjefe de la Misión ante la OEA
    Tel: (202) 234 - 2945
    Fax: (202) 265 - 4795

ECUADOR

José Ramón Jiménez Carbo
Procurador General del Estado - Presidente del Consejo Directivo del Consejo Nacional de Control de Sustancias Estupefacientes y Psicotrópicas (CONSEP)
    Tel: (593-2) 562 - 029/ 562-059
    Fax: (593-2) 562 - 060
    E-mail: rjimenez@pge.gov.ec

Henry Cucalón Camacho
Secretario Particular del Procurador General
    Tel: (593-2) 562 - 541/ 562 - 453
    Fax: (593-2) 562 - 060
    E-mail: hcucalon@pge.gov.ec

Alfredo Santoro Donoso
Secretario Ejecutivo del Consejo Nacional de Control de Sustancias
Estupefacientes y Psicotrópicas (CONSEP)
  Tel: (593) 222 - 1829
  Fax: (593) 256 - 4717
  E-mail: consep@uio.satnet.net

Alejandro Dávalos
Tercer Secretario – Embajada del Ecuador ante los Estados Unidos
  Tel: (202) 234 - 7200

EL SALVADOR

Francisco Bertrand Galindo
Ministro de Seguridad Pública y Justicia
  Tel: (503) 221- 1807
  Fax (503) 221- 3956
  E-mail: mjministro@telemovil.com

Juan Antonio Martínez Varela
Ministro de Defensa Nacional
  Tel: (503) 223 - 0233 / 298 - 1033
  Fax: (503) 298 - 2005
  E-mail: ministro.mdn@mail.nttcb.net

Alvaro Antonio Calderón Hurtado
General de División - Jefe del Estado Mayor Conjunto de la Fuerza Armada
  Tel: (503) 298 - 0880

Eduardo Hernández
Consejero – Representante Alterno de El Salvador ante la OEA
  E-mail: elsalvador.oea@erols.com

GRENADA

Augustine John
Minister of Education
  Tel: (473) 440 - 2166

Dave Alexander
Drug Avoidance Officer - Grenada National Drug Avoidance Committee
  Tel: (473) 440 - 7911
  E-mail: ndac@caribsurf.com

Denis G. Antoine
Ambassador, Permanent Representative of Grenada to the OAS
  Tel: (202) 265 - 2561
  Fax: (202) 265 - 2468
  E-mail: gdaemb@worldnet.att.net

GUATEMALA

Jorge Bolívar Díaz
Subsecretario Ejecutivo - SECCATID
Tel: (502) 331 - 0372 / 331- 1781
Fax: (502) 332 - 5385
E-mail: seccatid@gua.net

Manuel Fernando García-Robles
Primer Secretario – Representante Alterno de Guatemala ante la OEA
Tel: (202) 833 - 4015
Fax: (202) 833 - 4011
E-mail: gdaemb@worldnet.att.net

HONDURAS

Gladys Caballero de Arévalo
Designada a la Presidencia de la República, Presidenta del Consejo Nacional Contra el Narcotráfico
Tel: (504) 234 - 1480
Fax: (504) 230 - 5892
E-mail: cncn@ns.hondunet.net

Laura Elena Núñez de Ponce
Embajadora, Representante Permanente de Honduras ante la OEA
Tel: (202) 362 - 9656
Fax: (202) 537 - 7170
E-mail: honduras@oas.org

Ofelia Gutiérrez
Delegada por la CCP
Tel: (504) 234 - 1480
E-mail: cncn@ns.hondunet.net

Mario E. Chinchilla
Fiscal Especial de Lucha contra el Crimen Organizado del Ministerio Público
Tel: (504) 235 - 9396
Fax: (504) 235 - 9409
E-mail: informaticam@mphonduras.hn / chinchillaguerra53@yahoo.com

Ramón Custodio
Ministro de la Embajada de Honduras ante los Estados Unidos
Tel: (202) 362 - 9656
Fax: (202) 537 - 7170
E-miail: ramoncustodio@yahoo.com

Katyna Argueta Membreño
Representante Alterna de Honduras ante la OEA
Tel: (202) 362 - 9656
Fax: (202) 537 - 7170
E-mail: honduras@oas.org

JAMAICA

John A. Junor M.P.
Minister of Health
    Tel: (876) 967 - 0306
    Fax: (876) 922 - 8862
    E-mail: junorhmh@n5.com.jm

Charles Thesiger
Chairman – National Council on Drug Abuse (NDCA)
    Tel: (876) 927 - 2492 Ext.2234
    Fax: (876) 927 - 2116

Michael Tucker
Executive Director – National Council on Drug Abuse (NDCA)
    Tel: (876) 926 - 9002 ext. 4
    Fax: (876) 960 - 1820

MEXICO

Jorge Madrazo Cuéllar
Procurador General de la República - Procuraduría General de la República
    Tel: (525) 626 - 9100
    Fax: (525) 626 - 4419
    E-mail: ofproc@pgr.gob.mx

Mariano Herrán Salvatti
Fiscal Especial Antidrogas
    Tel: (525) 237 - 1830

Eduardo Ibarrola Nicolín
Subprocurador Jurídico y de Asuntos Legales Internacionales
    Tel: (525) 626 - 9255

Claude Heller
Embajador – Representante Permanente de México ante la OEA
    Tel: (202) 332 - 3663 / 332 - 3664
    Fax: (202) 332 - 9498

Alejandro Díaz de León
Attaché de la Procuraduría General de la República
    Tel: (202) 728 - 1734

Julian Ventura
Primer Secretario - Representante Alterno de México ante la OEA
    Tel: (202) 332 - 3663
    Fax: (202) 234 - 0602

NICARAGUA

María Alicia Duarte Bojorge
Secretaria Ejecutiva - Consejo Nacional de Lucha contra las Drogas
 Tel: (505) 228 - 5828/ 228 - 4115/ (505) 222 - 2011 (Secretaría Ejecutiva)
 Fax: (505) 228 - 7970
 E-mail: secejec@ibw.com.ni

PANAMA

José Antonio Sossa Rodríguez
Procurador General de la Nación - Comisión Nacional para el Estudio y la Prevención de los Delitos
Relacionados con Drogas (CONAPRED)
 Tel: (507) 227 - 0114 / 225 - 0250
 Fax: (507) 227 - 5249

Patricio Elías Candanedo
Fiscal Especial de Drogas - Procuraduría General de la Nación
 Tel: (507) 265 - 5630
 Fax: (507) 227 - 0114
 E-mail: patcan@mexico.com

Guillermo A. Ford
Embajador de Panamá ante los Estados Unidos
 Tel: (202) 483 - 1407
 Fax: (202) 483 - 8413

PARAGUAY

Domingo Guzmán Gaona
Secretario Ejecutivo Interino de la Secretaría Nacional Antidrogas (SENAD)
 Tel: (595-21) 202 - 672/ 202 - 679
 Fax: (595-21) 204 - 119
 E-mail: senad@sce.cnc.una.py

Cesar Núñez Alarcón
Asesor Jurídico Asuntos Internacionales - Secretaría Nacional Antidroga (SENAD)
 Tel: (595-21) 202 - 672/ 202 - 679
 Fax: (595-21) 204 - 119
 E-mail: senad@sce.cnc.una.py

Fernando Villaba Adorno
Director de Desarrollo Alternativo – Presidencia de la República Secretaría Nacional Antidroga
 Tel: (595-2) 120 - 2679
 Fax: (595-2) 120 - 4119
 E-mail: senad@sce.cnc.una.py

Juan Esteban Aguirre
Embajador del Paraguay ante los Estados Unidos
    Tel: (202) 483 - 6960

Diego Abente Brun
Embajador – Representante Permanente del Paraguay ante la OEA
    Tel: (202) 244 - 3003

Elianne Cibils
Consejera - Embajada del Paraguay ante los Estados Unidos
    Tel: (202) 483 - 6960
    E-mail: embapar@erols.com

Julio César Arriola
Ministro, Representante Alterno del Paraguay ante la OEA
    Tel: (202) 244 - 3003
    Fax: (202) 234 - 4508

PERU

Alejandro Aguinaga Recuenco
Ministro de Salud - Presidente de la Comisión de Lucha Contra el Consumo de Drogas (CONTRADROGAS)
    Tel: (511) 431- 0408
    Fax: (511) 431- 4648

Dennis del Castillo
Director de la Policía Nacional Antidrogas (DINANDRO)
    Tel: (511) 421 - 0813 / 221 - 7034
    Fax: (511) 421 - 4493
    E-mail: dilima@mail.cosapidata.com.pe / sec_lima@webperu.org.pe

María Teresa Hart
Ministra Consejera. Embajada del Perú ante los Estados Unidos
    Tel: (202) 833 - 9869
    Fax: (202) 659 - 8124
    E-mail: mthart@lepruwash.com

José Antonio García
Representante Suplente – Representación Titular del Perú ante la CICAD
    Tel: (202) 298 - 8336
    E-mail: cicadperu@aausaperu.org

REPUBLICA DOMINICANA

Marino Vinicio Castillo
Secretario de Estado y Presidente del Consejo Nacional de Drogas (CND)
(Dependencia del Poder Ejecutivo)
    Tel: (809) 221 - 8020/ 221 - 5166
    Fax: (809) 221 - 8019
    E-mail: cnac.drogas@codetel.net.do
                consejo@codetel.net.do

Diógenes A. Checo
Secretario Ejecutivo - Consejo Nacional de Drogas (CND)
(Dependencia del Poder Ejecutivo)
   Tel: (809) 221- 8020/ 221-5166
   Fax: (809) 221- 8019
   E-mail: cnac.drogas@codetel.net.do

Manuel Herrera
Director - PROPUID
   Tel: (809) 688 - 0777 / 221- 4747
   E-mail: PROPIUD@CODETEL.NET.DO

Ramón A. Quiñones
Ministro Consejero, Representante Alterno de la República Dominicana ante la OEA
   Tel: (202) 332 - 9142 / 332 - 6280
   Fax: (202) 265 - 8057

SAINT KITTS AND NEVIS

Earl Asim Martin
Minister of Health and Women's Affairs
   Tel: (869) 465 - 2521 ext. 1085
   Fax: (869) 465 - 8574
   E-mail: skandac@caribsurf.com

Izben C. Williams
Chairman – National Council on Drug Abuse Prevention
   Tel: (869) 465 - 2032
   E-mail: skandac@caribsurf.com

Kevin M. Isaac
Minister Counselor, Alternate Representative of Saint Kitts and Nevis to the OAS
   Tel: (202) 686 - 2626
   Fax: (202) 686 - 5740

SAINT LUCIA

Velon L. John
Minister of Legal Affairs, Home Affairs and Labour
   Tel: (758) 452 - 3622
   Fax: (758) 453 - 6315

Carol Mondesir
Director of the Substance Abuse Advisory Council Secretariat
   Tel: (758) 451 - 8990 / 453 - 0038
   Fax: (758) 453 - 1205
   E-mail: drugaps@candw.lc

Martha A. Auguste
First Secretary – Embassy of St. Lucia to the United States
    Tel: (202) 364 - 6792 / 364 - 6793
    Fax: (202) 364 - 6723
    E-mail: eofsaintlu@aol.com

SAINT VINCENT AND THE GRENADINES

St. Clair Thomas
Minister of Health and the Environment
    Tel: (809) 457 - 1745
    Fax: (809) 457 - 2684

Harold Rampersaud
Chief Medical Officer
    Tel: (784) 457 - 1873
    Fax: (784) 456 - 1646
    E-mail: ramps@caribsurf.com

Deborah Dalrymple
Director - Marion House (NGO)
    Tel: (784) 456 - 2161
    E-mail: mhouse@caribsurf.com

SURINAME

Chandrikapersal Santokhi
Police Commissioner and Head of the Judicial Department
    Tel: (597) 403 - 608
    E-mail: sanpoljd@sr.net

Prim Ritoe
Chairman of the National Anti-Drug Council
    Tel: (597) 472 - 923
    Fax: (597) 477 - 072

Henry L. Mac-Donald
Second Secretary – Alternate Representative of Suriname to the OAS
    Tel: (202) 244 - 2501
    Fax: (202) 244 - 5878
    E-mail: hmacdodyyy@aol.com

TRINIDAD AND TOBAGO

Joseph L. Theodore
Minister of National Security
    Tel: (868) 623 - 7579

Lancelot Selman
Director - Strategic Services Agency
Tel: (868) 625 - 8310
Fax: (868) 623 - 2526
E-mail: firebird@carib-link.net

John Sandy
Defense Attaché
Tel: (202) 467 - 6490
Fax: (202) 785 - 3130
E-mail: embbottobago@jslinks.com

UNITED STATES

Barry R. McCaffrey
Director
Office of National Drug Control Policy (ONDCP)
Executive Office of the President
Washington, D.C. 20500
Tel: (202) 395 - 6700
Fax: (202) 395 - 6708

Thomas Umberg
Deputy Director ONDCP
Office of National Drug Control Policy (ONDCP)
Executive Office of the President
Washington, D.C. 20500
Tel: (202) 395 - 6700
Fax: (202) 395 - 6708
E-mail:askncjrs@ncjrs.aspensys.com

Robert E. Brown, Jr.
Assistant Deputy Director
Office of National Drug Control Policy (ONDCP)
Executive Office of the President
Washington, D.C. 20500
Tel: (202) 395 - 6741
Fax: (202) 395 - 5197

Rand Beers
Assistant Secretary of State
Bureau of International Narcotics and Law Enforcement Affairs (INL)
Department of State
Tel: (202) 647 - 8464
Fax: (202) 736 - 4885

URUGUAY

Alberto Scavarelli
Viceministro de la Presidencia de la República, Secretario de la Junta Nacional de Prevención y Represión del Tráfico Ilícito Uso Abusivo de Drogas
    Tel: (598-2) 600 - 5445/ 200 - 9028
    Fax   (598-2) 487 - 3726

Eduardo Bouzout
Consejero - Representante Alterno del Uruguay ante la OEA
    Tel: (202) 333 - 0687
    Fax: (202) 337 - 3758

VENEZUELA

Mildred Camero
Presidenta de la Comision Nacional contra el Uso Ilícito de las Drogas (CONACUID)
    Tel: (58-2) 953 - 2851/ 953 - 2018/ 953 - 3918/ 953 - 5835
    Fax: (58-2) 953 - 0416
    E-mail: c.n.a.1@cantv.net
               c.n.a.2@cantv.net
               c.n.a.3@cantv.net

Rita Azuaje
Directora de la Comisión Nacional contra el Uso Ilícito de las Drogas (CONACUID)
    Tel: (58-2) 953 - 2851/ 953 - 2018/ 953 - 3918/ 953 - 5835
    Fax: (58-2) 953 - 0416
    E-mail: c.n.a.1@cantv.net
               c.n.a.2@cantv.net
               c.n.a.3@cantv.net

FRANCE

Jean-Paul Barré
Ambassador – Permanent Observer of France to the OAS
    Tel: (202) 686 - 5061
    Fax: (202) 244 - 9328

Thomas Erhardy
Deputy Police Attaché – Service de Cooperation Technique Internationale de Police
    Tel: (202) 944 - 6127
    Fax: (202) 944 - 6125

PORTUGAL

Antonio Jorge Mendes
Ambassador – Permanent Observer of Portugal to the OAS
Tel: (202) 328 - 8610
Fax: (202) 462 - 3726

Ana María Pires
Alternative Observer – Permanent Observer of Portugal to the OAS
Tel: (202) 328 - 8610
Fax: (202) 462 - 3726

SPAIN

Francisco Villar
Embajador – Observador Permanente de España ante la OEA
Tel: (202) 265 - 8365 - 66 / 332 - 0315
Fax: (202) 332 - 6889

Isabel Vicandi
Ministro - Observador Alterno de España ante la OEA
Tel: (202) 265 - 8365
Fax: (202) 332 - 6889

UNITED NATIONS OFFICE FOR DRUG CONTROL AND CRIME PREVENTION

Vincent McClean
Representative for United Nations Office for Drug Control and Crime Prevention
Tel: (212) 963 - 5631
Fax: (212) 963 - 4185
E-mail: mcclean@unorg

Organization of American States

César Gaviria, Secretary General

Camilo Granada, Assistant Secretary General

Inter-American Drug Abuse Control Commission (CICAD)

David R. Beall, Executive Secretariat

Alberto Hart, Assistant Executive Secretary

Ligia Guillén, Principal Secretary

Ana Chisman, Head Demand Reduction Section

Ruben Cobas, Inter-American Data Bank

Ruth Connolly, Head of Information Services

Angela Crowdy, GEG/MEM Support Unit

Federico Dafieno, National Commissions

Miguel Escudero, GEG/MEM Support Unit

Consuelo Fleming, GEG/MEM Support Unit

Rafael Franzini, Money Laundering Control

Amparo Hernandez, Travel Coordination

Marya Hynes, Inter-American Data Bank

Sofía Kosmas, GEG/MEM Support Unit

Nuala Lawlor, Intern of the Executive Secretariat

Ernesto Masaferro, Documents Technician

Ziggie Malyniwsky, Head of Supply and Reduction of Control

Katalina Montaña, Alternative Development

Carmen Ortega, Information Services

Marianne Parraud, Secretary

María Eugenia Pérez, Demand Reduction

Heidi Rauch, Demand Reduction

Herman Rincón, Legal Development

Jorge Ríos, Alternative Development

Joseph Rogers, Demand Reduction

Nelly Robinson, Administrative Support

Ana María Rollano, Technical Assistant

Javier Sagredo, National Commissions

Javier Seminario, Information Systems

Michael Sullivan, Head of Legal Development

Katia Tinajero-Montalvo, Supply Reduction and Control

Rosemary Gonzalez Vazquez, Events Organization

Franklin Zambrano, Head of Institution Building

Ricardo Zavaleta-Gerente, Head, Inter-American Data Bank

United States Interagency

Office of National Drug Control Policy

Barry R. McCaffrey, Director
Office of National Drug Control Policy

Janet Crist, Chief of Staff
Office of National Drug Control Policy

Dr. Vereen, Deputy Director
Office of National Drug Control Policy

Alejandra Y. Castillo, Policy Advisor
Office of National Drug Control Policy

Thomas Umberg, Deputy Director and Conference Moderator
Office of Supply Reduction
Office of National Drug Control Policy

Robert E. Brown, Assistant Deputy Director
Office of Supply Reduction
Office of National Drug Control Policy

Brad Hittle, Branch Chief Source Country Support
Office of Supply Reduction
Office of National Drug Control Policy

Mark Coomer, Branch Chief International Strategy/Programs
Office of Supply Reduction
Office of National Drug Control Policy

Hank Marsden, Director
Office of National Drug Control Policy

Richard Baum, Peru/Bolivia Policy Analyst
Office of Supply Reduction
Office of National Drug Control Policy

Allison Major, Colombia/Venezuela Policy Analyst
Office of Supply Reduction
Office of National Drug Control Policy

Robert Agresti, Europe/UNDCP Policy Analyst
Office of Supply Reduction
Office of National Drug Control Policy

Charlotte Sisson, Program Support Specialist
Office of Supply Reduction
Office of National Drug Control Policy

Suzanne Petrie, Mexico Policy Analyst
Office of Supply Reduction
Office of National Drug Control Policy

Chris Forbes, International Strategy/Programs Policy Analyst
Office of Supply Reduction
Office of National Drug Control Policy

Stuart Maberry, Deputy Director-Special Action Office
Office of Supply Reduction
Office of National Drug Control Policy

Steve Ritchie, Policy Analyst-International
Office of Supply Reduction
Office of National Drug Control Policy

Dave Shull, Assistant General Counsel
Office of National Drug Control Policy

Richard I. Kearsley, Defense Liaison
Office of Supply Reduction
Office of National Drug Control Policy

Brian London, U.S. Customs Liaison
Office of Supply Reduction
Office of National Drug Control Policy

Dirk A. Lamagno, DEA Liaison
Office of Supply Reduction
Office of National Drug Control Policy

Earl A. Burns, FBI Liaison
Office of Supply Reduction
Office of National Drug Control Policy

Daniel Schecter, Assistant Deputy Director
Office of Demand Reduction
Office of National Drug Control Policy

Javier Cordova, Prevention Policy Analyst
Office of Demand Reduction
Office of National Drug Control Policy

June Sivilli, Programs and Research Policy Analyst
Office of Programs, Budget, Research and Evaluations
Office of National Drug Control Policy

Kevin Whaley, Senior Advisor to the Director for State and Local Affairs
Bureau of State and Local Affairs
Office of National Drug Control Policy

Joseph Peters, Assistant Deputy Director
Bureau of State and Local Affairs
Office of National Drug Control Policy

Kurt F. Schmid , Director High Intensity Drug Trafficking Area HIDTA
High Intensity Drug Trafficking Area HIDTA
Office of National Drug Control Policy

George Kosnik, Branch Chief, Justice and Law Enforcement
Justice and Law Enforcement
Office of National Drug Control Policy

Brenda Bess, Justice & Law Enforcement Policy Analyst
Justice and Law Enforcement
Office of National Drug Control Policy

Paul Chabot, Analyst
Bureau of State and Local Affairs Policy Analyst
Office of National Drug Control Policy

Jaime Vega, Regions Policy Analyst
Office of National Drug Control Policy

Robert S. Weiner, Chief of Press Relations
Office of Public Affairs
Office of National Drug Control Policy

John Brennan, Public Affairs Specialist
Office of Public Affairs
Office of National Drug Control Policy

Shona Seifert, Senior Partner - Executive Group Director
ONDCP Media Campaign, Ogilvy & Mather

David McConnaughey, Senior Partner Management Supervisor
ONDCP Media Campaign, Ogilvy & Mather

Department of State

Thomas R. Pickering, Under Secretary Political Affairs
Department of State

Frank E. Loy, Under Secretary Global Affairs
Department of State

William Brownfield, Assistant Secretary Western Hemisphere Affairs
Department of State

Rand Beers, Assistant Secretary Bureau of International Narcotics and Law Enforcement Affairs
Department of State

Michael J. Senko, Director of Policy Coordination
Department of State

John M. Crow, Director Office of Latin Programs
Bureau of International Narcotics and Law Enforcement Affairs
Department of State

Elizabeth Carroll, Division Director, Office of Latin American and Caribbean Programs
Bureau of International Narcotics and Law Enforcement Affairs
Department of State

Daria Lyman, Caribbean Officer, Bureau of International Narcotics and Law Enforcement Affairs
Department of State

Scott Harris, Bureau of International Narcotics and Law Enforcement Affairs
Department of State

James Dudley, Country Officer for Paraguay and Uruguay, Bureau of Western Hemisphere Affairs
Department of State

Department of Defense

James E. Bodner, Principal Deputy Under Secretary
Office of the Under Secretary of Defense for Policy

Keith M. Huber, Director of Operations
U.S. Southern Command

Ana Maria Salazar, Deputy Assistant Secretary of Defense
Drug Enforcement Policy and Support

Jennie Lincoln, Project Director
U.S. Southern Command

Department of Justice

Mary Lee Warren, Deputy Assistant Attorney General
Department of Justice

Immigration and Naturalization Service

Doris Meissner, Commissioner
Immigration and Naturalization Service

Drug Enforcement Administration

Ronald E. Lard, Chief South American Operations
Drug Enforcement Administration

Laura Nagal, Chief Policy Strategic Planning
Drug Enforcement Administration

Federal Bureau of Investigation

W.K. Williams, Assistant Section Chief
Latin American Unit
Federal Bureau of Investigation

Department of Treasury

James E. Johnson, Under Secretary for Enforcement
Department of Treasury

United States Customs Service

Sam Banks, Deputy Commissioner of Customs
United States Customs Service

Charles E. Stallworth III, Executive Director Air Marine Division
United States Customs Service

Financial Crimes Enforcement Network

David M. Vogt, Assistant Director for Office of Research and Analysis
Financial Crimes Enforcement Network

Department of Transportation

Mary Bernstein, Director Drug and Alcohol Policy and Compliance
Office of the Secretary
Department of Transportation

United States Coast Guard

Admiral Ray Riutta, Rear Admiral U.S. Coast Guard
Department of Transportation

Crime and Narcotics Center

Joseph R. DeTrani, Director
Crime and Narcotics Center

James Stienger
Crime and Narcotics Center

National Drug Intelligence Center

Michael T. Horn, Director
National Drug Intelligence Center

Frank R. Shults, Chief Congressional and Interagency Relations
National Drug Intelligence Center

Substance Abuse and Mental Health Services Administration

Lorinda J. Daniel, Special Assistant to the Administrator
Substance Abuse and Mental Health Services Administration

National Institute on Drug Abuse

Dr. Alan Leshner, Director
National Institute on Drug Abuse

Patricia Needle
National Institute on Drug Abuse

Department of Education

Bill Modzeleski, Director Safe and Drug Free Schools Program
Department of Education

Santiago Summit Plan of Action – Narcotics Section

SANTIAGO SUMMIT OF THE AMERICAS
PLAN OF ACTION--NARCOTICS LANGUAGE –
Approved by Presidents on April 18, 1998

Prevention and Control of Illicit Consumption of and Traffic in
Drugs and Psychotropic Substances and other Related Crimes

Governments will:

-- *Continue* to develop their national and multilateral efforts in order to achieve full application of the Hemispheric Anti-Drug Strategy, and will strengthen this alliance based on the principles of respect for the sovereignty and territorial jurisdiction of the States, reciprocity, shared responsibility and an integrated, balanced approach in conformity with their domestic laws.

-- With the intention of strengthening mutual confidence, dialogue and hemispheric cooperation and on the basis of the aforementioned principles, develop, within the framework of the Inter-American Drug Abuse Control Commission (CICAD-OAS), a singular and objective process of multilateral governmental evaluation in order to monitor the progress of their individual and collective efforts in the Hemisphere and of all the countries participating in the Summit, in dealing with the diverse manifestations of the problem.

-- *Strengthen national efforts and international cooperation in order to:*

♦ Enhance their national policies and plans with regard to the prevention of illicit drug consumption, and step up measures, particularly at the community level, in schools and those aimed at the most vulnerable groups, such as children and young people, in order to prevent the growth and spread of this consumption and to eliminate financial incentives to illicit trafficking;

♦ Develop appropriate treatment, rehabilitation and reintegration programs with a view to alleviating the serious social effects, human suffering and other adverse effects associated with drug abuse;

♦ Increase cooperation in areas such as the collection and analysis of data, standardization of systems that measure illicit consumption, scientific and technical training and exchange of experiences;

♦ Develop or encourage the development of campaigns to foster greater social awareness of the dangers of drug abuse for individuals, the family and society as well as community participation plans;

♦ Sensitize public opinion as to the serious effects of drug abuse and the activities of criminal organizations that deal with them, including at the wholesale and retail level;

♦ Improve and update cooperative mechanisms to prosecute and extradite individuals charged with the traffic in narcotics and psychotropic substances and other related crimes, in accordance with international agreements, constitutional requirements, and national laws;

♦ Establish or strengthen existing, duly trained and equipped specialized central units responsible for requesting, analyzing and exchanging among the competent State authorities information relating to the laundering of the proceeds, assets and instrumentalities used in criminal activities (also known as money laundering);

♦ Reinforce international and national control mechanisms to impede the illicit traffic and diversion of chemical precursors;

♦ Promote the rapid ratification and entry into force of the Inter-American Convention Against the Illicit Production and Trafficking of Firearms; promote the approval and prompt application of the Model Regulations on the Control of Arms and Explosives Connected with Drug Trafficking of CICAD; encourage States, that have not already done so, to adopt the necessary legislative or other measures to ensure effective international cooperation to prevent and combat illicit transnational traffic in firearms and ammunition, while establishing, or strengthening, systems to enhance the tracing of firearms used in criminal activity; and

♦ Eliminate illicit crops through the increased support of national alternative development programs as well as eradication and interdiction.

-- Strengthen national drug control commissions, with a view to improving coordination in each country in the planning and implementation of their respective national plans and in streamlining international assistance in this area.

--Underscore the valuable contribution of civil society, through its different organizations, in the areas of prevention of illicit consumption, treatment, rehabilitation, and social reintegration of drug addicts.

--Encourage financial institutions to redouble their efforts to prevent money laundering and the appropriate business sectors to strengthen its controls to prevent the diversion of chemical precursors.

--Give full support to the upcoming Special Session of the United Nations General Assembly which will be held in June 1998 for the purpose of promoting international cooperation with respect to illicit drugs and related crimes and encourage all States to participate actively, at the highest level, in that international meeting. They will make every effort to ensure effective implementation of international narcotics agreements to which they have subscribed, at regional and sub-regional levels, and for these to operate in consonance with the hemispheric effort and reaffirm their support for CICAD and its fundamental role in the implementation of these agreements.

The Multilateral Evaluation Mechanism (MEM)

Background

At CICAD's twenty-second regular session in November 1997 in Lima, Peru, the Delegation of Honduras proposed the creation of a multilateral evaluation mechanism which would make periodic recommendations to member states on improving their capacity to control drug trafficking and abuse and enhance multilateral cooperation. The United States similarly proposed the multilateralization of the inter-American drug control effort. After discussion, the Commission agreed to convene consultative meetings in Washington, D. C. to analyze these proposals, taking into account the interventions of other delegations, and decide on the procedure for designing a multilateral mechanism consistent with the Anti-Drug strategy in the Hemisphere adopted by CICAD in Buenos Aires and signed in Montevideo in December 1996.

When they met at their Second Summit, in April 1998 in Santiago, Chile, the Heads of State and Government of the Americas turned this concept of multilateral evaluation into a mandate, declaring in the Plan of Action that their countries would undertake the following:

"Continue to develop their national and multilateral efforts in order to achieve full application of the Anti-Drug Strategy in the Hemisphere, and will strengthen this alliance based on the principles of respect for the sovereignty and territorial jurisdiction of the States, reciprocity, shared responsibility and an integrated, balanced approach in conformity with their domestic laws; With the intention of strengthening mutual confidence, dialogue and hemispheric cooperation and on the basis of the aforementioned principles, develop, within the framework of the Inter-American Drug Abuse Control Commission (CICAD-OAS), a singular and objective process of multilateral governmental evaluation in order to monitor the progress of their individual and collective efforts in the Hemisphere and of all the countries participating in the Summit, in dealing with the diverse manifestations of the problem."

Based on these mandates and in order to execute them, the twenty-third regular meeting of CICAD (May 1998) formed an Intergovernmental Working Group on the Multilateral Evaluation Mechanism (IWG-MEM). Dr. Jean Fournier, the Principal Representative of Canada, was elected to chair the Group, with Dr. Pablo Lagos, the Principle Representative of Chile, as Vice Chair. In conformity with the decisions adopted at the Second Summit of the Americas and in the earlier consultative meetings of CICAD, the IWG-MEM focussed in its initial discussions on the principles, objectives and the general characteristics of a multilateral evaluation mechanism.

Objective of the MEM

The objective of the MEM is directly to strengthen mutual confidence, dialogue and hemispheric cooperation in order to deal with the drug problem with greater efficacy. It will follow-up on the progress of individual and collective efforts of all the countries participating in the Mechanism, indicating both results achieved as well as obstacles faced by the countries.

The Multilateral Evaluation Process

Though the design of the mechanism is not complete at this point, it is possible to highlight what advances in the discussion may produce. Countries to be evaluated would provide data in response to a standard questionnaire. Each country would also present a document prepared by its government on the situation of the country's drug problem. This document would illustrate achievements made by the country, as well as the difficulties it faces and areas in which cooperation should be strengthened.

The indicators designed for the questionnaires are divided into five main categories: National Plans and Strategies; Prevention and Treatment; Reduction of Drug Production; Law Enforcement Measures; and the Cost of the Drug Problem. These indicators should serve as tools for measuring national and hemispheric efforts and results to combat illicit drug use, production, and trafficking. They can provide feedback on how nations are meeting goals in a wide range of areas, including the development of anti-drug strategies and national plans, drug seizure operations, the creation of prevention and rehabilitation programs, reductions in illicit crop production, diversion of precursor chemicals, prevention of money laundering and arms trafficking, among others.

A Governmental Experts' Group (GEG) made up of experts from all 34 member states would use the results of the questionnaire, and the summary document presented by each government to carry out evaluations on a country-by-country basis. Final evaluation drafts would be submitted to the Commission for consideration and approval. The GEG would be responsible for the 34 individual multilateral evaluations and the hemispheric report, together with recommendations on how to strengthen cooperation and the capacity of States to address the drug problem as well as to stimulate technical assistance and training programs as part of overall anti-drug efforts.

A first evaluation round of all CICAD member states is planned for 2000. This first evaluation is based on 61 indicators and would show its results in 2001 for presentation at the Third Summit of the Americas in Québec City, Canada that same year.

Principles of the MEM Process

◆ Respect for sovereignty, territorial jurisdiction, and the domestic laws of States
◆ Reciprocity, shared responsibility and an integrated balanced approach to this issue
◆ Observance of the Anti-Drug Strategy in the Hemisphere and international agreements and instruments in force

Characteristics of the MEM

◆ Governmental, singular and objective with the participation of specialized representatives of the governments
◆ Transparency, impartiality and equality to assure an objective evaluation
◆ Full and timely participation of the States based upon mutually and previously established rules and procedures of general application to guarantee an equitable evaluation process The exclusion of sanctions of any kind
◆ Respect for the confidentiality of the deliberations and the information provided by States, in accordance with established norms and procedures

MEM Indicators

OEA/Ser.L/XIV.4.5
CICAD/MEM/doc.12/99 rev. 1
June 15, 1999
Original: English

FIFTH MEETING OF THE INTERGOVERNMENTAL
WORKING GROUP ON THE MULTILATERAL
EVALUATION MECHANISM (IWG-MEM)
May 3-7, 1999 Washington, D.C.

INDICATORS FOR THE FIRST EVALUATION ROUND
TO BE CARRIED OUT IN 2000

131

INDEX

GOAL 1: OPTIMIZE NATIONAL STRATEGY

SPECIFIC OBJECTIVE: A. To establish a framework to guide all anti-drug activities.
SPECIFIC OBJECTIVE: B. To have a national system for drug information collection and analysis.

GOAL 2: PREVENT DRUG USE AND TREAT DRUG ABUSERS

SPECIFIC OBJECTIVE: C. To have national guidelines for the reduction of the demand of drugs.
SPECIFIC OBJECTIVE: D. To have a national system of drug abuse prevention that targets key populations.
SPECIFIC OBJECTIVE: E. To have a national system of treatment, rehabilitation and social reintegration of drug abusers that includes different modalities.
SPECIFIC OBJECTIVE: F. Prevention and treatment: Training
SPECIFIC OBJECTIVE: G. Evaluation of the impact/effectiveness of drug abuse prevention, treatment and rehabilitation programs

GOAL 3: REDUCE DRUG PRODUCTION

SPECIFIC OBJECTIVE: H. Cultivation/ production reduction
SPECIFIC OBJECTIVE: I. To have alternative development programs to complement law enforcement actions and promote new legal productive activities.
SPECIFIC OBJECTIVE: J. To prevent diversion of pharmaceuticals and controlled chemical substances used for the illicit manufacture of drugs.

GOAL 4: IMPROVE DRUG CONTROL AND RELATED MEASURES

SPECIFIC OBJECTIVE: K. To stem and / or eliminate illicit drug trafficking
SPECIFIC OBJECTIVE: L. To decrease firearms diversion related to drug trafficking
SPECIFIC OBJECTIVE: M. To prevent, control and repress money laundering

GOAL 5: ESTIMATE THE COST THAT THE DRUG PROBLEM REPRESENTS FOR THE COUNTRIES.

SPECIFIC OBJECTIVE N. To identify the ability of the countries to quantify the cost of the drug problem.

GOAL 1: OPTIMIZE NATIONAL STRATEGY

SPECIFIC OBJECTIVE A: To establish a framework to guide all anti-drug activities.

INDICATORS	SCOPE OR DEFINITION
1. Existence of National Anti-drug Plan	**Plan Covers:** ▪ **Supply reduction** ▪ **Demand reduction** ▪ **Control measures** ▪ **Institutional structure** ▪ **Budget** ▪ **Evaluation System**
2. Existence of Central Coordinating body	**Areas including:** ▪ **Supply reduction** ▪ **Demand reduction** ▪ **Control measures** ▪ **Information center**
3. Existence of budget for Central Coordinating Body	**Budget for the functioning of the Central Coordinating Body**

133

INDICATORS	SCOPE OR DEFINITION
4. Ratified international Conventions	**Relevant international multilateral, regional, and bilateral agreements:** - **UN Convention Against Illicit Traffic in Narcotic Drugs and Psychotropic Substances, 1988** - **UN Convention on Psychotropic Substances, 1971** - **UN Convention on Narcotic Drugs, 1961** - **Inter-American Convention on Mutual Assistance in Criminal Matters** - **Inter-American Convention Against Corruption** - **Inter-American Convention Against the Illicit Manufacturing of and Trafficking in Firearms, Ammunition, Explosives and other Related Materials**
5. Existence of national laws and/or regulations according to international conventions/ agreements and CICAD model regulations for the control of chemical substances, money laundering and firearms.	**Areas covered:** - **Supply reduction** - **Consumption/ prevention/ treatment** - **Control measures[1]**

SPECIFIC OBJECTIVE B: To have a national system for drug information collection and analysis.

INDICATORS	SCOPE OR DEFINITION
6. Existence of a system of compilation and maintenance of statistics and documentation.	**System contemplates:** - **Supply reduction** - **Demand reduction, (including a national standardized system of epidemiological surveys of drug use, as well as qualitative research)** - **Control Measures** - **Societal impact of illicit drugs.**

134

---

[1] Includes drug trafficking, money laundering, firearms, and chemical controls.

GOAL 2: PREVENT DRUG USE AND TREAT DRUG USERS

SPECIFIC OBJECTIVE C: To have national guidelines for the reduction of the demand of drugs.

INDICATORS	SCOPE OR DEFINITION
7. Existence of a national demand reduction strategy.	

SPECIFIC OBJECTIVE D: To have a national system of drug abuse prevention that targets key populations.

INDICATORS	SCOPE OR DEFINITION
8. Existence of drug abuse prevention programs that target key populations, and if available, percentage coverage.	The programs cover: a) school- based b) community-based c) street children d) prisoners and prison authorities e) out-of-school youth f) other groups at risk according to each country's assessment
9. Existence of "drugs in the workplace" programs.	Includes prevention education and employee assistance programs
10. Adoption of the Guiding Principles of Drug Demand Reduction of the UN Political Declaration, New York, June 1998, and its Plan of Action, approved March 1999.	Consideration of these principles and the Plan of Action in the design and execution of demand reduction programs

SPECIFIC OBJECTIVE E: To have a national system of treatment, rehabilitation and social reintegration of drug abusers that includes different modalities.

INDICATORS	SCOPE OR DEFINITION
11. Existence of guidelines on minimum standards of care for drug treatment established by each member state	"Minimum standards of care": the regulation of drug treatment facilities to assure quality care and the protection of human rights
12. Existence of programs concerning: a) early intervention b) outreach c) treatment, d) rehabilitation e) reintegration into the community	with consideration for: • different treatment modalities • various populations as targeted • the involvement of "civil society"

SPECIFIC OBJECTIVE F: Prevention and treatment: Training

INDICATORS	SCOPE OR DEFINITION
13. Existence of professional specialized training in drug abuse prevention and treatment	Training may be offered nationally or sub-regionally.

SPECIFIC OBJECTIVE G: Evaluation of the impact/effectiveness of drug abuse prevention, treatment and rehabilitation programs

136

INDICATORS	SCOPE OR DEFINITION
14. Regular diagnosis of drug use in the general population, and methodology used to measure it	General population surveys: often achieved through a national sample of households. A similar estimate might be achieved through "mall intercepts" [2] or focus groups. Measuring trends over time requires that the same methodology be used in consecutive years.

INDICATORS	SCOPE OR DEFINITION
15. Existence of research on prevention and drug use, and of evaluations of drug abuse prevention programs.	
16. Average age of first use of any illicit drug	Measuring the change over time and working toward a net increase in average age of first use
17. Annual incidence of new drug users.	Measuring the change over time and working toward a net decrease in the annual incidence of new drug use.
18. Existence of studies to evaluate various treatment and rehabilitation programs and modalities in order to assess their effectiveness	Research that measures the extent to which people in drug treatment stay drug free

---

[2] The sample should have the same distribution by age and by sex.

GOAL 3: REDUCE DRUG PRODUCTION

SPECIFIC OBJECTIVE H: Cultivation/ production reduction

INDICATORS	SCOPE OR DEFINITION
19. Area under cultivation (Hectares), and potential production capacity (metric tons) by year (by plant type).	"Area under cultivation" considers those areas that are not officially designated as traditional growing areas. *Does not include indoor cultivation* "Production capacity" is calculated using the area under cultivation (hectares) and the plant density (number of plants per hectare). In the case of marijhuana, the average weight of a plant (defined by the country) will be used to calculate the total potential production (plant matter) measured in metric tons. In the case of coca and poppy, the area under cultivation and plant density will be used in conjunction with an average factor (defined by the country) regarding the quantity of final drug product that can be produced per plant.
20. Number of plants seized from indoor cultivation and potential production capacity by year (by plant type).	In the case of indoor cultivation of marijhuana, the production capacity will be calculated using the total number of plants and the average weight of a plant (defined by the country) resulting in the total theoretical capacity measured in metric tons of plant material.
21. Hectares eradicated, abandoned or otherwise removed from illicit cultivation by year (by plant type).	It is understood that various means can be used to achieve a reduction in cultivation based upon national policies and programs. These include eradication, spraying, and abandonment.
22. New areas of illicit cultivation by year (by hectare) (by plant type).	

INDICATORS	SCOPE OR DEFINITION
23. Reduction in production of illicit synthetic drugs produced with chemical substances, by year (by drug).	Measured by examining chemical seizures "Illicit synthetic drugs" are those not produced from organic matter, but synthesized using chemicals or precursors
24. Illicit laboratories destroyed per year (by organic and synthetic drugs produced) and the quantities of drugs that could have been produced in the laboratory	The term "laboratories" refers to facilities or locations where drugs are produced, manufactured or otherwise prepared (including processing pits). These drugs include organic based substances such as cocaine, heroin, hashish etc as well as synthetic drugs such as amphetamine-like stimulants, methamphetamine and "designer drugs".

SPECIFIC OBJECTIVE I: To have alternative development programs to complement law enforcement actions and promote new legal productive activities.

INDICATORS	SCOPE OR DEFINITION
25. Existence of Alternative Development programs (by type)	"Alternative development", as defined by the CICAD Expert Group, is "A process to prevent and eliminate the illicit cultivation of plants containing narcotic drugs and psychotropic substances through specifically designed rural development measures in the context of sustained national economic growth and sustainable development efforts in countries taking action against drugs, recognizing the particular socio-cultural characteristics of the target communities and groups, within the framework of a comprehensive and permanent solution to the problem of illicit drugs."
26. Number of economic development projects coordinated and operating in Alternative development areas, by year[3]	Enables to determine the efficiency and tendencies of alternative development activities
27. Number of families benefiting from the alternative development projects by year	Allows for the measurement of the effectiveness of alternative development programs and their social impact

SPECIFIC OBJECTIVE J: To prevent diversion of "pharmaceuticals"[4] and controlled chemical substances[5] used for the illicit manufacture of drugs.

---

[3] In the observation section of this indicators, the amount of funds allocated per-capita (from national and foreign sources) on alternative development projects are included

[4] 'Pharmaceuticals' means those substances defined in the U.N. Conventions 1961 (as amended in 1972) and 1971 that are legally distributed for use in medical and scientific purposes. Statistical information on the number of persons arrested, tried etc. for illegally trafficking in these substances is included in the replies to indicators 42, 43 and 44.

[5] Includes chemical substances listed in CICAD's Model Regulations.

INDICATORS	SCOPE OR DEFINITION
28. Existence of a national body for the control and prevention of diversion of a) Pharmaceuticals b) Controlled chemical substances	This could be an entity which carries out both controls or two separate entities Each body coordinates implementation of national chemical control system and/or pharmaceuticals, which includes a registry of companies, import/export licenses, and control of transport system
29. Existence of a system to estimate legitimate annual national needs of: (a) Pharmaceuticals; (b) Controlled chemical substances	"Legitimate annual national needs" relates to the substances and quantities required for the production of psychoactive pharmaceutical drugs used for therapeutic medical purposes and for chemicals using for industrial, commercial, or manufacturing purposes. This also takes into consideration transit and re-export operations.
30. Existence of a mechanism to regulate professions concerned with the use and distribution of pharmaceuticals	"Professions" includes pharmacists, physicians, dentists and veterinarians
31. Existence of a mechanism for effecting operational information exchange and collaboration among national authorities with responsibilities for: a) Pharmaceuticals; b) Controlled chemical substances	"Mechanism" could include routine operational contacts and activities, a task force, or a communications system among national chemical and/or pharmaceutical control authorities

141

INDICATORS	SCOPE OR DEFINITION
32. Existence of a centralized agency for effecting information exchange and collaboration between countries, in relation to: a) Pharmaceuticals; b) Controlled chemical substances	
33. a)Existence of national laws and/or regulations for penal, civil and administrative sanctions against the diversion of i) Pharmaceuticals; ii) Controlled chemical substances b) Number of applications of sanctions under such national laws and/or regulations by type and by regulated group, by year	
34. Number of pre-export notifications, by year, sent by the competent authority of the exporter country to the chemical control competent authorities of the importer, and transit country.	Prior notice of individual exports is used as a means to identify end-users of the consignment
35. Percentage of pre-export notifications replied on time relative to the number of pre-export notifications received, by year.	The period for a timely response is 15 days
36. Quantities of i) pharmaceuticals; ii) controlled chemical substances. Seized and disposed of by substance, by volume, and by year	"Disposed of" includes destruction, dilution, neutralization, landfill, incineration, and sale. Includes substances contained in the tables of the CICAD's Model regulations and pharmaceuticals
37. Number of requests made for cooperation, during the last year, based on international cooperation agreements on chemical control, and the number of replies	Includes international cooperation such as multilateral and bilateral maritime/ riverine agreements, mutual assistance agreements and MOU's.

142

GOAL 4: IMPROVE DRUG CONTROL AND RELATED MEASURES

SPECIFIC OBJECTIVE K: To stem and / or eliminate illicit drug trafficking

INDICATORS	SCOPE OR DEFINITION
Existence of administrative, judicial and law enforcement agencies specifically responsible for investigating, controlling and/or eliminating illicit drug trafficking.	"Law enforcement agencies " includes police, customs, and others. "Drug trafficking" is as defined in Article 3, paragraphs 1 and 2 of the 1988 U.N. Convention.
38. EXISTENCE OF A MECHANISM FOR EFFECTING COORDINATION, COOPERATION AND TIMELY EXCHANGES OF INFORMATION AMONG NATIONAL AUTHORITIES.	"Mechanism" could include routine operational contacts and activities, a task force, or a communications system or network among national authorities
39. Existence of a centralized agency for effecting coordination, cooperation and timely exchanges of information between countries in accordance with international agreements.	
40. a) Number of drug seizure operations by law enforcement agencies, by year. b) Quantities of drugs seized by law enforcement agencies, by substance, volume and by year	"Seizure" means temporarily prohibiting the transfer, conversion, disposition or movement of property on the basis of an order issued by a competent authority
41. Number of persons arrested for illicit drug trafficking, by offence, by year[6] (other than for possession of drugs for personal use).	

---

[6] The reply should be indicated as a percentage of the total population of the country. The reply should also indicate to what extent these arrests, charges and convictions disrupted major criminal organizations.

INDICATORS	SCOPE OR DEFINITION
42. Number of persons charged[7] for illicit drug trafficking relative to number of arrests, by offence, by year (other than for possession of drugs for personal use).	
43. Number of persons convicted[8] for illicit drug trafficking relative to number of persons charged, by offence, by year, other than for possession of drugs for personal use.	
44. Taking account of international agreements, in the last year, the number of requests made for international cooperation to investigate and prosecute illicit drug trafficking and the number of replies.	"international agreements" include bilateral and multilateral agreements, mutual legal assistance treaties, and MOU's.

---

[7] Idem
[8] Idem

144

SPECIFIC OBJECTIVE L: To decrease firearms diversion related to drug trafficking.

INDICATORS	SCOPE OR DEFINITION
45. EXISTENCE OF NATIONAL LAWS AND/OR REGULATIONS, THAT: (A) CRIMINALIZE ILLICIT MANUFACTURE AND ILLICIT TRAFFICKING OF FIREARMS, AMMUNITION, EXPLOSIVES AND OTHER RELATED MATERIALS; (B) ESTABLISH ADMINISTRATIVE CONTROL MEASURES TO PREVENT THE OFFENCES REFERRED TO IN PARAGRAPH (A); (C) AUTHORIZE THE FREEZING OR SEIZURE OF FIREARMS, AMMUNITION, EXPLOSIVES AND OTHER RELATED MATERIALS; AND (D) AUTHORIZE CONFISCATION OR FORFEITURE OF THE OBJECTS REFERRED TO IN PARAGRAPH (C).	The terms "illicit manufacturing", "illicit trafficking", "firearms", "ammunition", "explosives", "other related materials", and "administrative control measures" used in this indicator take their meaning from Article I of the Inter-American Convention and Article 1.3 of the Model Regulations for the Control of the International Movement of firearms, their Parts, Components and Ammunition (hereinafter "the OAS/CICAD Model Regulations"). The terms "freezing" or "seizure" mean temporarily prohibiting the transfer, conversion, disposition or movement of property or temporarily assuming custody or control over property on the basis of an order issued by a court or other competent authority, and "confiscation " or "forfeiture" refer to the permanent deprivation of property effected by a court or other competent authority together with their disposal in the manner set out in Article VII (2) of the Inter-American Convention.

INDICATORS	SCOPE OR DEFINITION
46. Existence of a mechanism (or mechanisms) and/or an authority (or authorities)	"Mechanism" could include routine operational contacts and activities, a task force, or a communications system or network
(a) that maintains a record by dates, classification-description and numbers of firearms, ammunition, explosives and other related materials manufactured, imported, exported or moving in-transit through that country,	The terms "manufacturing", "importation", "exportation", and "in-transit shipment" used in this indicator take their meaning from Article I of the Inter-American Convention and Article 1.3 of the OAS/CICAD Model Regulations.
(b) that ensures, before authorizing the release for export of shipments of firearms, ammunition, explosives and other related materials that importing or in-transit countries have issued the necessary licenses or authorizations,	
(c) that effects inter-agency coordination an information exchanges at the national level,	
(d) that serves as a centralized point for effecting coordination and information exchanges among states.	

146

INDICATORS	SCOPE OR DEFINITION
47. Number of persons	
(a) Charged[9] for illicit manufacturing and trafficking of firearms, ammunition, explosives and other related materials, by offence, by year, and	
(b) Convicted[10], relative to number of persons charged, by offence, by year	
48.	**"Seizure"** means temporarily prohibiting the transfer, conversion, disposition or movement of property on the basis of an order issued by a competent authority. **"Confiscation"** or **"forfeiture"** refer to the permanent deprivation of property effected by a court or other competent authority together with their disposal in the manner set out in Article VII (2) of the Inter-American Convention. The **"type"** of firearm refers to its descriptive classification as provided for by the OAS/CICAD Firearms Model Regulations.
a) Number of seizure operations [11] in relation to firearms, ammunition, explosives and other related materials by law enforcement agencies, by year.	
b) Quantities of firearms, ammunition, explosives and other related materials seized by law enforcement agencies, by type and by year.	
c) Quantities of firearms, ammunition, explosives and other related materials confiscated or forfeited by competent authorities by type and by year.	
d) Identification of the origins and routing employed in the diversion of the seized firearms, ammunition, explosives and other related materials.	

---

[9] The reply with respect to this indicator should also reflect what the numbers of persons charged are as a percentage of the total population of the country. The reply should also indicate to what extent these charges and convictions disrupted major criminal organizations. The reply could also make reference to the nature of these organizations, their modus operandi; the means used to divert the firearms, ammunition, explosives and other related materials and other pertinent circumstances

[10] The reply with respect to this indicator should also reflect what the numbers of persons convicted are as a percentage of the total population of the country. The reply should also indicate to what extent these charges and convictions disrupted major criminal organizations. The reply could also make reference to the nature of these organizations, their modus operandi; the means used to divert the firearms, ammunition, explosives and other related materials and other pertinent circumstances

[11] Wherever possible the reply should indicate those cases which are related to illicit drug trafficking. Otherwise, the reply should simply reflect all firearms, ammunition, explosives and other related materials forfeited.

INDICATORS	SCOPE OR DEFINITION
49. Taking account of international agreements, in the last year, the number of requests made for international cooperation to investigate and prosecute the illicit manufacturing and trafficking of firearms, ammunition, explosives and other related materials and the number of replies.	"International agreements" include bilateral and multilateral agreements, mutual legal assistance treaties, and MOU's.

148

SPECIFIC OBJECTIVE: M. To Prevent, control and repress money laundering [12]

INDICATORS	SCOPE OR DEFINITION
50. Existence of national laws and/or regulations that criminalizes money laundering and national laws and/or regulations that provide for administrative controls to prevent money laundering [13]	"Money Laundering" refers to the offenses described in Article 2 of the CICAD/OAS Model Regulations Concerning Laundering Offences Connected to Illicit Drug Trafficking and related Offences. "Administrative controls" refers to financial regulations issued by Central Banks and Banking Superintendencies.
51. Existence of national laws and/or regulations that authorize the freezing or seizure and forfeiture of assets related to money laundering. [14]	The terms "freezing" or "seizure" mean temporarily prohibiting the transfer, conversion, disposition or movement of property or temporarily assuming custody or control of property on the basis of an order issued by a court or other competent authority. "Forfeiture" means the permanent deprivation of proceeds effected by a court or other competent authority.

INDICATORS	SCOPE OR DEFINITION
52. Existence of a central agency responsible for receiving, requesting, analyzing and disseminating to competent authorities, disclosures of information relating to financial transactions and that allows for the exchange of operational information and operational collaboration among national authorities and among related central agencies in other countries.	Such central agencies internationally known as Financial Intelligence/ Investigation Units (FIUs) are provided for in the Model Regulations.

---

[12] The Summit of the Americas Plan of Action of Buenos Aires sets out the hemispheric basis of indicators for money laundering control measures.

[13] This refers to financial regulations issued by Central Banks and Banking Superintendencies.

[14] The reply should indicate if the country has national laws and/or regulations providing for other means of seizing and forfeiting proceeds of crime, such as, for example, extinguishment of title or civil forfeiture.

53. Existence of national laws and/or regulations requiring financial institutions and others responsible to report suspicious or unusual transactions to competent authorities and to comply with other control measures in accordance with national law.	**"Financial institutions" and "others responsible" are as defined in Articles 9 and 16, respectively, of the Model Regulations.** **"Suspicious or unusual transactions" includes** transactions that have no apparent economic or lawful purpose or that are inconsistent with those normally associated with a particular enterprise as referred to in Article 13 of the Model Regulations. **"Other control measures" are as described in Articles 10 to 15 of the Model Regulations.**
54. Existence of a mechanism or entity for the management and/or distribution of assets seized and/or forfeited from illicit drug trafficking.	*"Mechanism" could include routine operational contacts and activities, a task force or a communications system or network to prevent, control and repress money laundering.*
55. Number of persons arrested[15] for money laundering, by year.	
56. Number of persons charged [16] relative to persons arrested for money laundering, by year.	
57. Number of persons convicted[17] relative to persons charged for money laundering, by year	

---

[15] The reply should be indicated as a percentage of the total population of the country. The reply should also indicate to what extent these arrests, charges and convictions disrupted major criminal organizations.
[16] idem
[17] idem

INDICATORS	SCOPE OR DEFINITION
58. Number of administrative and/or regulatory sanctions applied by supervisory agencies against financial institutions and others responsible, as well as judicial sanctions for failure to report suspicious transactions and other failures to comply with their legal responsibilities in relation to money laundering control.	"Administrative/regulatory sanctions" include fines, increased reporting requirements, restrictions on activities and loss of the licenses or charters that authorize financial institutions to carry on business. "Judicial sanctions" means those imposed by a court of law according to the laws of each country. "supervisory agencies" refers to the government authorities responsible for the supervision of financial institutions, such as, for example, central banks, superintendencies of banks, the federal reserve, and government agencies responsible for overseeing other financial institutions' activities such as insurance companies, the stock market, gambling activities and others. "Financial institutions" and "others responsible" means those identified in Articles 9 and 16 of the OAS/CICAD Model Regulations to Control Money Laundering.
59. Taking account of international agreements, in the last year, the number of requests made for international cooperation to investigate and prosecute money laundering and the number of replies.	"international agreements" includes bilateral and multilateral agreements, mutual legal assistance treaties, and MOU's.

151

GOAL 5: ESTIMATE THE COST THAT THE DRUG PROBLEM[18] REPRESENTS FOR THE COUNTRIES.

SPECIFIC OBJECTIVE O: To identify the ability of the countries to quantify the cost of the drug problem.

INDICATORS	SCOPE OR DEFINITION
60. Existence of a system to assess the human, social and economic costs related to the drug problem.	The countries with these systems in place, may provide quantitative information related to: a) Human resources assigned to the prevention and control of the drug problem; b) Financial resources used and percentage of the national budget assigned to these activities; c) Amount of international economic as well as other types of assistance received to be directly or indirectly assigned to these activities; d) Number of persons killed and disabled (individualized by officials and non officials); e) Health costs, such as mortality, morbidity, accidents (traffic, workplace, etc.); f) Other social costs

[18] The illicit cultivation, production, manufacture, sale, demand, trafficking and distribution of narcotic drugs and psychotropic substances, including amphetamine-type stimulants, the diversion of precursors, and related criminal activities.